Webster's New World

DICTIONARY OF COMPUTER TERMS

Compiled by

Laura Darcy and Louise Boston

K

SIMON & SCHUSTER, INC.

Copyright © 1983 by Simon & Schuster, Inc.

All rights reserved
including the right of reproduction
in whole or in part in any form

Published by New World Dictionaries/Simon and Schuster
A Division of Simon & Schuster, Inc.
Simon & Schuster Building
Rockefeller Center
1230 Avenue of the Americas
New York, New York 10020

*Dictionary Editorial Offices: New World Dictionaries,
850 Euclid Avenue, Cleveland, Ohio 44114*

SIMON AND SCHUSTER, TREE OF KNOWLEDGE, WEBSTER'S
NEW WORLD and colophons are trademarks of
Simon & Schuster, Inc.

Manufactured in the United States

10 9 8 7 6 5 4

0-671-46866-9

Library of Congress Cataloging in Publication Data
Main entry under title:

Webster's new world dictionary of computer terms.

    1. Computers—Dictionaries. 2. Electronic data
processing—Dictionaries. I. Darcy, Laura. II. Boston,
Louise. III. Title: New world dictionary of computer
terms.
QA76.15.W37 1983   001.64'03'21   83-9415

FOREWORD

Amazing and exciting, confusing and frustrating, and, above all else, an undeniable presence in our lives. Love them or hate them, computers are entering everyone's life. On the desk, in the car, and across the counter at the bank, computers are performing certain tasks for people thousands of times more quickly and efficiently than the best of human minds. And yet, even though these devices are encountered daily, most people are still unfamiliar with how they work and with the basic terminology used in the computer industry. All of a sudden, due to the rapid advancements in technology, "bits" and "bytes," "hardware" and "software," are terms that must be understood by all of us so that we may function more effectively in the business world, in scientific activities, in academic studies, and in discussions with our school-age children.

Unfortunately, the proliferating literature dealing with computers often assumes that the reader is familiar with the various terms used in the field. Anyone uncertain of their meanings can quickly get lost in the maze of jargon and buzzwords employed by more experienced computer users.

This dictionary has been compiled in an effort to provide brief but precise definitions for those terms most commonly encountered in the computer industry today. Wherever possible, technical terms have been avoided so that the definitions might be easily read and understood. Where a proper understanding of a term depends upon the comprehension of another term, the reader is directed to it by a cross-reference, set in small capital letters. The main goal of the compilers of this work has been to provide newcomers to the computer field with definitions for those terms they are most likely to read or hear. This work is also intended to provide a quick reference for those terms that even the more experienced computer user may be uncertain of.

All terms are entered in a strict alphabetical listing, so that spaces and dashes are to be ignored in looking up a particular word or phrase. A term that begins with a number is entered in the position it would occupy if the number had been spelled out, for example, **80-column card** appears in the position for "eighty-column card."

The most common meaning has been provided for most words. Frequently, the same word will have other, more specific meanings when used in specialized fields within the computer industry. If a term has more than one commonly accepted meaning, or is used as more than one part of speech, each sense is preceded by a number. Wherever possible, the more general sense of the word appears first. Because so many of the terms have been recently introduced, absolute standardization of meaning has not yet taken place, so that varying with the area of the country and the field within the computer industry in which it is used, one term may have several similar, yet slightly different meanings.

Where synonyms exist, one term had to be selected, sometimes arbitrarily, as the entry at which the definition is supplied. The synonym or synonyms are entered in their own alphabetical locations and are simply cross-referred to the term with the definition. The synonym appears in boldface, as do all main entries, and is followed by the term, printed in small capitals, that contains the definition. Any word appearing in small capitals within a definition is, in effect, also a cross-reference.

Any term appearing in regular capitals or in light boldface has not been entered separately with a definition, but its meaning is self-evident or is explained within the context in which it is being used. Other terms whose definitions may help to flesh out a meaning are set in small capitals after the definition proper, preceded by "See" or "Compare." Many illustrative examples have been included with the definitions to help clarify the meaning, often by detailing frequently encountered situations in data processing.

The terminology of computer science, like that of other modern sciences, is characterized by an abundance of acronyms, and the most frequently encountered ones have been entered here, with the phrases from which they are formed. Since acronyms are printed and spoken as words, where the pronunciation may not be self-evident, it has been supplied in a simple, easily read key. A number of abbreviations, and of slang and other informal terms, commonly used by computer personnel have been entered and defined.

The use of computers will certainly continue to grow. People in all walks of life will become increasingly dependent upon them. A common understanding, among lay and professional users, of the basic terms of the technology will need to be achieved. This dictionary is designed as a tool to help bring that understanding about.

Provided in the back of the dictionary are conversion tables useful for quick reference. Included are tables converting decimal numbers to the corresponding binary, hexadecimal, and octal numbers; a special table for easy conversion of larger numbers from decimal to hexadecimal or hexadecimal to decimal; a table of powers of two and another for the powers of sixteen; a table that converts EBCDIC characters to their equivalent binary and hexadecimal codes; and, lastly, a table that converts ASCII characters to their equivalent binary and hexadecimal codes.

In compiling this dictionary, the editors found the vast resources of the Cleveland Public Library to be invaluable, as were the advice and knowledge provided by manufacturers and by a number of very talented colleagues in the Computer Services Department of Cleveland State University

Laura Darcy
Louise Boston

A

A 1 in the HEXADECIMAL NUMBER SYSTEM, the symbol that corresponds to the decimal number 10 **2** abbreviation for ACCUMULATOR

abend acronym for **ABNORMAL END** OF TASK **1** a programming or machine error that occurs during execution of a program and that recovery routines are unable to resolve, so that a programming task is terminated before it is completed **2** to so terminate the execution of a program

abnormal end of task ABEND

abort to terminate the execution of a program because of an abend and to return control to the operating system

absolute address the number, label, or name that is assigned by the engineer to an actual storage location in main memory when the computer is designed and that may be used in a program to refer to a specific location Compare RELATIVE ADDRESS, SYMBOLIC ADDRESS

absolute code programs or instructions in which absolute addresses are used to store data in or retrieve data from main memory

absolute loader a loader that brings an OBJECT PROGRAM into fixed, predetermined addresses in main memory for execution: an absolute loader reads the object code statement that contains the starting address of the instructions and loads the instructions into successive storage locations starting at that address

ACC abbreviation for ACCUMULATOR

access   **1** to store data in, or retrieve it from, storage   **2** the ability to so store or retrieve data

access arm   a mechanism that supports and positions one or more READ–WRITE HEADS on a disk

access mechanism   the mechanism that supports the access arms on a disk drive and moves them in unison over the disk recording surface

access method   a programming technique for storing and retrieving data between main memory and an input/output device

accessory   a peripheral device, such as a disk drive

access time   **1** the length of time required to store or retrieve data between main memory and an external storage device: access time for data stored on disk is calculated by taking the sum of the SEEK TIME and ROTATIONAL DELAY time and is used in predicting the amount of time a given application will need to access a file. The access time for data stored on tape depends on the physical location of the data on the tape, since a specific record can only be accessed by first accessing all the data that precedes it in the file   **2** the length of time required to access a word in main memory

accumulator   a register in the ALU used for arithmetic operations and for loading and storing data between the CPU and main memory: for example, the accumulator performs an add operation by adding an incoming number to its contents and replacing its contents with the sum

accumulator register   ACCUMULATOR

accuracy   the degree to which the result of an arithmetic operation is free from error: for example, a three–digit number that is correctly computed is accurate, whereas a four–digit number that is incorrectly computed is inaccurate but has greater precision Compare PRECISION

accuracy control character a COMMUNICATIONS CONTROL CHARACTER indicating that an error in data transmission has occurred, that the data sent is to be disregarded, or that the data cannot be represented on the receiving device

ACK clipped form of ACKNOWLEDGE CHARACTER

acknowledge character 1 a COMMUNICATIONS CONTROL CHARACTER transmitted by the receiving device to the sending device to indicate that the data sent has been received correctly **2** ACCURACY CONTROL CHARACTER

acknowledgment in data communications, the transmission of acknowledge characters from the receiving device to the sending device, indicating that the data sent has been received correctly

ACM abbreviation for ASSOCIATION FOR COMPUTING MACHINERY an association formed to advance the development of information processing as a science and to promote the exchange of information among professionals and the public

acoustic coupler a type of modem that provides the communication between a remote terminal and the computer by converting data into a sequence of tones and transmitting the tones over standard telephone lines. The tones are reconverted to binary digits by a modem at the receiving station: the acoustic coupler is connected by inserting a standard telephone handset into two rubber cups that are attached directly to the terminal or to a separate modem

acronym a word formed from the first (or first few) letters of each of a group of words: for ex-

ample, COBOL for **CO**MMON **B**USINESS ORI-
ENTED **L**ANGUAGE

action an operation in the computer resulting
from an instruction

active program any program currently being executed in the computer

activity ratio the percentage of records that have
been accessed during the execution of a program relative to the total number of records in
the file

actual decimal point a decimal point that actually occupies a position in a numeric field Compare ASSUMED DECIMAL POINT

ADC abbreviation for ANALOG–TO–DIGITAL CON-
VERTER

ADCCP abbreviation for ADVANCED DATA COM-
MUNICATION CONTROL PROTOCOL a standard,
BIT–ORIENTED PROTOCOL developed by the Ameri-
can National Standards Institute (ANSI) See HDLC

adder a LOGIC DEVICE that performs the arithmetic
addition of two binary numbers See FULL–ADDER,
HALF–ADDER

adder–subtracter a LOGIC DEVICE in the CPU that
computes and outputs the result of an addition
or subtraction operation

add–on circuits, systems, or hardware devices that
can be attached to a computer to increase its
memory or improve its performance

address 1 a label, name, or number that identifies
a particular register, an exact storage location in
main memory, or an external storage device **2**
that part of the operand of an instruction that
identifies a specific location in memory **3** to
store data in, or retrieve it from, a specific location in memory

addressable designating storage locations in main memory that can be directly accessed through an instruction

address bus a bus that carries the address of data from the CPU to main memory or to an external storage device See SYSTEM BUS

addressing mode a method for storing and retrieving data in main memory: different types of computers offer a variety of different addressing modes See RELATIVE ADDRESSING, INDIRECT ADDRESSING, DIRECT ADDRESSING, IMMEDIATE ADDRESSING

address modification the use of a particular addressing mode to alter an address contained in an instruction: for example, an address can be altered by adding a number to it so that it then contains the address of the next sequential storage location in main memory

address part that portion of an INSTRUCTION that specifies an address

address register a register that is used to hold an address

add time the time it takes the computer to add two numbers, not including the time required to retrieve the numbers to be added and to store the sum

administrative data processing that field of electronic data processing that is concerned with the financial or managerial aspects of a business Compare SCIENTIFIC DATA PROCESSING

ADP abbreviation for AUTOMATIC DATA PROCESSING

advanced data communication control protocol ADCCP

AFIPS (AY fips) acronym for **A**MERICAN **F**EDERATION OF **I**NFORMATION **P**ROCESSING **S**OCIETIES an organization formed of representatives from various data processing societies to advance knowledge in the field and to represent the societies on a national level

algebraic hierarchy parentheses parentheses that determine the order in which the various components of a mathematical expression will be evaluated: for example, the parentheses in the expression ((A + B) x C) / D specify that the sum A + B will be formed, multiplied by C, and the product will be divided by D

ALGOL acronym for **ALGO**RITHMIC **L**ANGUAGE a high–level, procedure–oriented programming language used internationally for scientific computations: many variations of ALGOL exist, such as ALGOL10, ALGOL60, and ALGOL68

algorithm a predetermined set of instructions for solving a specific problem in a finite number of steps Compare HEURISTIC

alias **1** an alternate LABEL **2** an alternate ENTRY POINT in main memory for the start of execution of a program **3** an alternate name for a member of a PARTITIONED DATA SET

allocate to assign a resource to a TASK: the operating system controls the assignment of the resource

allocation see RESOURCE ALLOCATION, DYNAMIC STORAGE ALLOCATION, STORAGE ALLOCATION, STATIC STORAGE ALLOCATION

alphabetic referring to data that consists of letters and special symbols

alphameric ALPHANUMERIC

alphanumeric contraction of ALPHABETIC–NUMERIC referring to data that consists of numbers and alphabetic characters

alterable memory READ–WRITE MEMORY

alternate routing in data communications, the process of switching the path between two locations to an alternate when the normal path is not available

alternate track a track on a DIRECT ACCESS STORAGE DEVICE that is assigned to replace a defective primary track for the storage of data Compare PRIMARY TRACK

ALU abbreviation for ARITHMETIC–LOGIC UNIT the portion of the CPU that performs arithmetic and logical operations

AM abbreviation for AMPLITUDE MODULATION

American National Standards Institute ANSI

amplitude modulation a MODULATION technique in which the amplitude of a signal is varied to differentiate between a binary 1 and 0

analog referring to the representation of numerical quantities by the measurement of continuous physical variables: for example, the magnitude of an electrical signal might represent a number Compare DIGITAL

analog computer a computer that performs its tasks by measuring continuous physical variables (e.g., pressure, voltage, length, flow), manipulating those physical variables to obtain a solution, and transforming the solution into a numerical equivalent: usually it is a special–purpose computer designed to solve a scientific or technical application Compare DIGITAL COMPUTER

analog data continuous data represented by physical variables, such as pressure, voltage, length, or flow Compare DIGITAL DATA

analog–to–digital converter a device that measures an analog signal and converts it to digital form Compare DIGITAL–TO–ANALOG CONVERTER

analyst a computer specialist who defines a problem and develops algorithms for its solution See SYSTEMS ANALYST, PROGRAMMER ANALYST

ancillary equipment PERIPHERAL DEVICE

AND 1 a LOGICAL OPERATOR connecting two propositions, each of which may be either true or false, that results in a new proposition. If both propositions are true, the new proposition is true: for example, in the statement, "IF A=1 AND B=1 THEN C=1," both A and B must be equal to one for C to equal one; otherwise C is equal to zero **2** designating such an operation

AND gate a gate that produces an output signal of binary 1 when both input signals are 1; otherwise, the output signal is 0

annotation a comment or descriptive remark added to a program or flowchart

ANSI acronym for **A**MERICAN **N**ATIONAL **S**TANDARDS **I**NSTITUTE a nongovernmental organization that proposes, modifies, approves, and publishes data processing standards for voluntary use in the United States

answerback the process of transmitting a COMMUNICATIONS CONTROL CHARACTER from a receiving device to the sending device, indicating readiness to accept data, acknowledge the receipt of data, or identify itself

AP abbreviation for ATTACHED PROCESSOR

APL abbreviation for A PROGRAMMING LANGUAGE a high-level, procedure-oriented programming language used for mathematical and scientific computations: APL is a powerful, concise language that has an unusual syntax and character set. Programming in APL generally requires the use of a special terminal keyboard that contains keys specific to the APL language

append to add to the end: for example, to add additional data to the end of an existing file

application a system, such as a payroll, that has been defined to be suitable for electronic data processing techniques

application program a program designed to solve a particular problem for an application, such as a payroll program

applications programmer a person who writes programs for the solution of an application

approximation the resulting value when a number is rounded to a specified decimal place during an arithmetic operation

architecture the composite of specific components and the way in which they interact, that forms a computer system

area search a search for those records in a file that are part of a specified group, such as those of employees from a particular department

argument **1** PARAMETER **2** a variable whose value determines the value of a mathematical function: for example, in the function $y = 2x + 6$, x is an argument whose value determines the value of y

arithmetic pertaining to computing by adding, subtracting, multiplying, or dividing

arithmetic expression an expression formed by combining any number of variables, constants, arithmetic operators, and paired parentheses, that can be reduced to a single numeric value: for example, $x = 2a + (b-4)/2$

arithmetic instruction an instruction that tells the computer to perform an arithmetic operation

arithmetic–logic unit ALU

arithmetic operation the addition, subtraction, multiplication, or division of numerical quantities

arithmetic operator a symbol used in an arithmetic expression to indicate the type of arithmetic operation to be performed: the standard operators are + (add), − (subtract), * (multiply), and / (divide)

arithmetic register a dedicated register in the ALU used for arithmetic and logical operations

arithmetic relation two arithmetic expressions separated by one of the RELATIONAL OPERATORS: $a+b > c+d$ is an example of an arithmetic relation

arithmetic shift a SHIFT that multiplies or divides the contents of a register by a power of its base number: for example, the arithmetic shift of a binary number one position to the right multiplies the number by 2^1; the arithmetic shift one position to the left divides the number by 2^1

arithmetic statement ARITHMETIC INSTRUCTION

arithmetic unit ALU

arm ACCESS ARM

array a group of two or more logically related elements identified by a single name: generally stored in consecutive storage locations in main memory

array index number a number that identifies a specific element in an array

artificial intelligence the area of study in computer science concerned with the development of a machine that can engage in humanlike thought processes, such as reasoning, learning, and self-correction

artificial language a language whose syntax and rules were explicitly developed prior to usage: computer programming languages, such as COBOL and PASCAL, are artificial languages Compare NATURAL LANGUAGE

ascending sort a sorting technique that arranges items in a lowest to highest sequence

ASCII (ASS kee) acronym for **A**MERICAN **S**TANDARD **C**ODE FOR **I**NFORMATION **I**NTERCHANGE a standard seven–bit code almost always transmitted with a PARITY BIT (for a total of eight bits per character), that was established by the American National Standards Institute to achieve compatibility between various types of data processing and data communications equipment: ASCII is the most commonly used code for non–IBM equipment

ASR abbreviation for AUTOMATIC SEND/RECEIVE

assemble to translate symbolic code into equivalent machine code

assembler a program that translates symbolic code into its equivalent machine code and usually produces an ASSEMBLY LISTING

assembler directive PSEUDO–INSTRUCTION

assembly the process of translating a program written in symbolic code into its equivalent machine code: the time during which this process occurs is called **assembly time**

assembly language a low–level programming language that uses mnemonic instructions, such as STO for store and SUB for subtract, instead of binary numbers that represent the corresponding machine language instruction: assembly languages are written to correspond to a specific computer's machine language

assembly language instruction an instruction written in assembly language that consists of an optional label, an OP code, and an operand

assembly listing the printed output from an assembler: the assembly listing displays the SYMBOLIC CODE adjacent to the corresponding MA-

CHINE CODE, a table of the symbols used in the program, and any diagnostics that result from errors detected in the translation process

assembly program ASSEMBLER

assignment operator an operator used in an assignment statement that causes the value on the right to be placed into the variable on the left of the operator: the assignment operator is the equal sign (=)

assignment statement a programming statement that gives a value to a variable, as in $x = x + 1$, as well as to a constant, as in $x = 2$

associative memory a type of memory for retrieving data by comparing a key to the contents of each storage location (rather than by the address of the location) until the desired item is found: the key is a copy of all or part of the data being retrieved. Associative memory may be used in main memory, scratchpad memory, or cache memory or for other types of memory in which a rapid search is required

associative storage ASSOCIATIVE MEMORY

assumed decimal point a decimal point that does not actually occupy a position in a numeric field but is implied to be present for calculations: a number that has an assumed decimal point rather than an actual decimal point is stored more efficiently since storage space is not required for the decimal point Compare ACTUAL DECIMAL POINT

asynchronous computer a computer in which a signal indicates when an operation is completed and also serves as the signal to begin another operation, so that the operations do not start and stop at regular, timed intervals Compare SYNCHRONOUS COMPUTER

asynchronous device a device that transmits signals at irregular intervals to the system with which it is communicating Compare SYNCHRONOUS DEVICE

asynchronous time–division multiplexing a time–division multiplexing technique in which only those terminals with data to transmit are allotted a period of time in which to do so Compare SYNCHRONOUS TIME–DIVISION MULTIPLEXING

asynchronous transmission a method of transmission that allows data to be sent at irregular intervals by preceding each character with a START BIT and following it with a STOP BIT Compare SYNCHRONOUS TRANSMISSION

ATDM abbreviation for ASYNCHRONOUS TIME-DIVISION MULTIPLEXING

atom a basic element in a list: in LIST PROCESSING LANGUAGES, the term **atom** usually refers to one item in a list: for example, in the list "the little brown dog," each word is an atom

atomic symbol ATOM

attached processor a processor connected to a main computer in order to assist in performing tasks: an attached processor is not equal in capacity to a main processor and cannot perform all tasks if the main computer fails

attended operation the operation of a computer system that requires an operator to provide manual intervention when necessary: for example, an operator may have to manually mount a tape on a tape drive when it is called for by the operating system

attention key a function key on a terminal that signals the HOST COMPUTER to interrupt execution of the current task, as in interrupting the listing of a file

attenuation a reduction in amplitude of a signal during data transmission: attenuation is caused by resistance in the communication line and may cause loss of data

attribute a characteristic that describes data: a typical attribute would be the length of a record in a file

automatic check a test performed by a hardware device in the computer to verify the accuracy of the transmission, manipulation, or storage of data Compare PROGRAMMED CHECK

automatic coding an AUTOMATIC PROGRAMMING technique in which a program, such as an assembler, is used to prepare machine code from symbolic code

automatic data processing DATA PROCESSING in which machines are used to perform a series of operations on data, thus reducing the need for human intervention Compare ELECTRONIC DATA PROCESSING

automatic error correction a communications method for detecting errors in data transmission when they occur and allowing for the retransmission or correction of the data by means of ERROR–CORRECTING CODE

automatic interrupt INTERRUPT

automatic message switching a MESSAGE SWITCHING technique that automatically routes incoming messages to an appropriate destination by means of information contained in the message itself

automatic programming the process of using a program to prepare another program: a GENERATOR PROGRAM is an example of automatic programming

automatic recovery program a program that takes control during a hardware failure and attempts to keep the computer functioning: an automatic recovery program may keep only basic functions operational or may switch control to a backup system

automatic send/receive a teletypewriter that can punch and read paper tape off–line and can transmit data either from a keyboard or paper tape: used especially with small business computers Compare KEYBOARD SEND/RECEIVE

automation any of various ways of implementing systems by means of mechanical or electronic machines to eliminate the need for manual processing

auxiliary equipment PERIPHERAL DEVICE

auxiliary memory AUXILIARY STORAGE

auxiliary operation OFF–LINE OPERATION

auxiliary storage ON–LINE storage, other than main memory, such as disk or tape

availability the ratio of time a device is operating correctly to the total scheduled time for operating

average latency the amount of time it takes to rotate the recording surface on a DIRECT ACCESS STORAGE DEVICE one half its full rotation: average latency is expressed in milliseconds and can be used in estimating the amount of time required to access a file

B

B in the HEXADECIMAL NUMBER SYSTEM, the symbol that corresponds to the decimal number 11

background the teleprocessing or multiprogramming environment in which lower–priority tasks are processed during a time when higher–priority tasks are inactive Compare FOREGROUND

background program a lower–priority program that can be executed when higher–priority tasks are inactive Compare FOREGROUND PROGRAM

backing storage AUXILIARY STORAGE

backplane MOTHERBOARD

backup 1 designating hardware, software, or data that can be made available in case of failure or unavailability of the primary system **2** to so duplicate hardware, software, or data

backup copy a duplicate of the original version of data or software that is made in case the original is destroyed: backup copies are usually duplicated on a different storage medium: for example, if a file stored on disk is not accessible because of a disk drive malfunction, a backup copy stored on a different medium, such as tape, would still be available

Backus–Naur form a notational convention used in describing the syntax of a programming language, developed by John Backus and Peter Naur: used in specifying those symbols that constitute a syntactically valid program in a given programming language

BAL acronym for BASIC ASSEMBLY LANGUAGE a simplified version of an assembly language

balanced system a computer system in which the number of computations being performed by the CPU is equal to the number of input/output operations being performed Compare COMPUTE-BOUND, I/O–BOUND

BAM acronym for BASIC ACCESS METHOD

band **1** a range of wavelengths or frequencies **2** CHANNEL (sense 1)

band printer CHAIN PRINTER

bandwidth a measure of the range of frequencies, at or near maximum power levels, that a communication line can transmit: expressed in hertz

bar code a code consisting of a number of magnetic ink lines that are imprinted on a label in varying widths and can be read with a scanning device: often used, as in Universal Product Codes, to record information at the point of sale in a retail store for controlling inventory

bar printer an IMPACT PRINTER that prints a line of FULLY FORMED CHARACTERS by striking TYPE BARS, located side by side in every print position, against an inked ribbon and paper. Each type bar contains all the characters in a particular character set and moves vertically until the correct character is in place. Once all the characters for a line are positioned, the entire line is printed See LINE PRINTER

barrel printer DRUM PRINTER

base number the number of digits available in each position of a number system: for example, the base number for the DECIMAL NUMBER SYSTEM is 10, since there are 10 available digits for each position (0, 1, 2, 3, 4, 5, 6, 7, 8, 9). In the BINARY NUMBER SYSTEM, the base number is 2, since there are 2 digits available for each position (0, 1)

base point RADIX POINT

base register **1** INDEX REGISTER **2** a nonaddressable register that is used to convert a RELATIVE ADDRESS to an ABSOLUTE ADDRESS. The absolute address of the first WORD of a program is stored in the base register and is automatically added to the addresses of storage locations referenced in the program; this converts the relative address (relative to the beginning word of the program) to an absolute address (the actual address) See RELATIVE ADDRESS

BASIC acronym for **B**EGINNER'S **A**LL–PURPOSE **S**YMBOLIC **I**NSTRUCTION **C**ODE a programming language that is easy to learn and widely used as the first programming language taught in schools and as the principal language in many minicomputers and microcomputers. It is commonly used on terminals where each programming statement is entered on the keyboard and immediately executed by the computer. The response sent back to the terminal allows the programmer to detect errors quickly and make decisions. Although it is simple to use, it contains many advanced features for handling mathematical formulas and character strings

basic access method any ACCESS METHOD in which each request in a program to store or retrieve data causes a corresponding input/output operation to occur

basic direct access method an ACCESS METHOD in which a record within a block of data stored on a DIRECT ACCESS STORAGE DEVICE can be accessed directly by specifying either an address relative to the beginning of the block where the search for the record begins or the actual address of the record

basic indexed sequential access method an ACCESS METHOD in which a record in a block of data stored on a DIRECT ACCESS STORAGE DEVICE can be accessed directly by using an index that contains the keys and corresponding addresses for each record within the block

basic partitioned access method an ACCESS METHOD in which sequences of data are accessed as individual members on a DIRECT ACCESS STORAGE DEVICE: a directory identifies the member name and the address where the member begins. This access method is also used to store and retrieve programs in a program library

basic sequential access method an ACCESS METHOD in which data is organized sequentially in blocks: when the program specifies that the data is needed, execution is suspended until storage or retrieval of the data is completed

basic telecommunications access method an ACCESS METHOD in which data can be directly stored in or retrieved from main memory by using a terminal

batch 1 a group of all the instructions and data relevant to a program, or a number of similarly grouped programs, to be input to the computer for processing in a single run **2** to so group a program or programs

batch compiler a compiler that translates all the statements in a program at one time, rather than line by line Compare INTERACTIVE COMPILER

batch processing 1 the processing of an individual program, that does not permit interaction between the program and user once the program has been read by the computer Compare INTERACTIVE PROCESSING **2** the efficient processing of a collection of related programs grouped together as a single run: for example, the batch processing of a series of FORTRAN programs would be executed by the FORTRAN compiler as a single JOB STREAM See COMPILE-AND-GO

battery backup system a system, generally used with minicomputers or microcomputers having volatile memory, that goes into effect to protect data during a power failure

baud a unit of measurement that denotes the number of discrete SIGNAL ELEMENTS, such as bits, that can be transmitted per second: for example, a device that transmits 300 bits per second can also be said to transmit at 300 baud. The word **baud** is derived from the surname of J.M.E. Baudot (1845–1903), a French pioneer in the field of printing telegraphy and the inventor of the Baudot code

Baudot code a code used in communications in which each character transmitted is represented by five bits

B-box INDEX REGISTER

BCD code abbreviation for BINARY–CODED DECIMAL CODE **1** a standard six–bit code (with a seventh bit used as a PARITY BIT) for the representation of characters: the six bits permit the representation of 64 characters, including letters, numbers, and special symbols   Compare ASCII, EBCDIC **2** a code for the representation of decimal numbers in which each decimal digit is represented by a four–bit binary number: for example, the decimal number 17 is represented as 0001 0111 with the bit positions weighted, from left to right, 8–4–2–1. In binary notation, the decimal number 17 is represented as 10001

BDAM (BEE dam) acronym for BASIC DIRECT ACCESS METHOD

beginning–of–tape marker a marker used to indicate the point on a magnetic tape where the recording of information may begin: it is generally a reflective strip, about an inch in length, that is sensed photoelectrically when it passes over a light beam on the tape drive and is usually located about eight feet from the beginning of the tape

benchmark program a standardized computer program used to test the processing power of a computer relative to other computers: a benchmark program can be designed to solve generalized problems, called **benchmark problems,** such as file processing, sorting, or mathematical computations, or to solve a more specific problem that will account for much of the use of that computer. The performance, as of processing speed, can be evaluated and compared to that of other computers tested with the same program. This process is called a **benchmark test** and can be used as a comparison tool in purchasing a computer

bias in mathematics, the difference between an estimated value of a statistic, such as a mean, and the true value

bidirectional bus a bus that transfers data to and from the CPU on a single circuit Compare UNIDIRECTIONAL BUS

bidirectional flow the transfer of data in either direction between two flowchart symbols: bidirectional flow is represented by a single FLOWLINE

bidirectional printing printing of lines of output on a printer in alternate directions, so that a line printed from left to right is followed by one printed from right to left: bidirectional printing increases efficiency by eliminating carriage return delays

billibit KILOMEGABIT

billicycle KILOMEGACYCLE

billisecond NANOSECOND

binary **1** referring to the base 2 number system in which the digits 1 and 0 are used **2** referring to a condition where there are only two possible choices: for example, typical conditions may be thought of as **on** or **off**, **true** or **false**, **yes** or **no**

binary arithmetic operation an arithmetic operation in which the operands and the result are represented in binary notation

binary card a standard punch card on which each of the 960 punch positions available can represent a 0 or 1. Each column of twelve punch positions is interpreted as having an upper and lower half of six punch positions each. The binary arrangement of zeros and ones in each half column represents a number, character, or special symbol: one binary card can store 160 bytes of information. Binary cards are never punched with a KEYPUNCH, but they can be punched by a computer using an attached CARD PUNCH

binary cell MEMORY CELL

binary chop BINARY SEARCH

binary code any code using bits to represent numbers, characters, and/or special symbols, such as ASCII, EBCDIC, or BCD: each computer has a type of binary code that is used to represent machine instructions and data

binary–coded decimal code BCD CODE (sense 1)

binary–coded decimal notation BCD CODE (sense 2)

binary counter a counter that is increased (or decreased) by binary 1 with each input pulse

binary digit BIT

binary dump a dump that is in binary representation instead of the usual hexadecimal representation

binary loader ABSOLUTE LOADER

binary number a number in the binary number system represented by one or more bits

binary number system the base 2 number system that represents a binary number as the sum of successive powers of two: for example, the binary number 1011 can be expressed as $(1 \times 2^3) + (0 \times 2^2) + (1 \times 2^1) + (1 \times 2^0)$, where $2^0 = 1$, and is equivalent to the decimal number 11

binary operation DYADIC OPERATION

binary operator DYADIC OPERATOR

binary point a point that separates the integer portion of a binary number from the fractional portion: for example, the binary number 101.01 can be expressed as $(1 \times 2^2) + (0 \times 2^1) + (1 \times 2^0) + (0 \times 2^{-1}) + (1 \times 2^{-2})$, where $2^0 = 1$, and is equivalent to the decimal number 5.25

binary search a search method in which a sorted list of records is successively halved until the desired record is located: a binary search is performed on a list of n records by first determining the midpoint of the list, determining which half holds the desired record, and discarding the other half. The process is repeated on the remaining half, and so on, until the desired record is located. The midpoint is determined by n/2. When n is an odd number, the midpoint is most commonly determined by rounding the result to the next highest integer Compare SEQUENTIAL SEARCH

binary synchronous communication BISYNC

binary–to–decimal conversion the process of converting a binary (base 2) number to the equivalent decimal (base 10) number

binary–to–hexadecimal conversion the process of converting a binary (base 2) number to the equivalent hexadecimal (base 16) number

binary–to–octal conversion the process of converting a binary (base 2) number to the equivalent octal (base 8) number

binary tree a DATA STRUCTURE in which the first node (record) is called the root: all subsequent nodes branch to the right when their key is less than that of a previous node and to the left when it is greater. Each record is stored with the keys of those records to its right and with those to its left so that a record can be found by tracing the keys from the root through subsequent nodes

binary variable a variable that can assume one of two values (**true** or **false**, 1 or **0**)

binding time the instant when a symbol or an expression has been translated into machine code and assigned an address of a storage location in main memory

bipolar designating integrated circuits used in chips requiring transistors having two poles and two current carriers: such circuits are of a higher speed because of a lower current density than MOSFET circuits

biquinary code a seven–bit code for the representation of decimal digits, in which the first two bits are paired to represent five or zero and the last five bits are used to represent the numbers 0, 1, 2, 3, or 4. Together the seven bits represent the integers 0 through 9. The bit positions are weighted, from left to right, 50 43210: for example, the number 7 is represented as 10 00100

BISAM (BYE sam) acronym for **B**ASIC **I**NDEXED **SE**QUENTIAL **A**CCESS **M**ETHOD

bistable referring to a hardware device that has the ability to assume only two stable states, **on** or **off**, **1** or **0**, etc.

bistable device an elementary device in the computer having two stable states, such as a flip—flop or a magnetic core

BISYNC acronym for **BINARY SYNC**HRONOUS COMMUNICATION an IBM character—oriented protocol used for the synchronous transmission of binary—coded data between two devices, that uses a defined set and sequence of control characters

bit contraction of **B**INARY DIGIT a digit in the binary number system represented by a 0 or a 1: a bit is the smallest unit of storage in the computer. Groups of bits form other units of storage such as a nibble, byte, or word

bit density BPI

bit manipulation the process of setting individual bits in a word to the desired states (binary 1 or 0)

bit—oriented protocol a PROTOCOL that uses a unique BIT PATTERN representing a flag character to separate distinct groups of data bits

bit—parallel designating or using the technique of PARALLEL TRANSMISSION

bit pattern a group of bits consisting of a predetermined number of bits and forming a binary number: for example, in EBCDIC, each bit pattern consists of eight bits that form a binary number and uniquely identifies a character

bit rate the number of bits transmitted in a specified length of time: bit rate is usually expressed in bits per second

bit—slice processor a CPU that is constructed from individual chips, each of which contains a section of a complete ALU, the multiplexers, and data paths using a four—bit format, that can be combined to form a CPU with a greater word length: usually for custom–designed, special–purpose microprocessors

bit stream a bit string that is transmitted over a communication line with no separations between the character groups

bit string a sequence of related bits

blank character a character, or bit pattern, arbitrarily chosen to produce a space in data

blind to set a device so that it does not receive unwanted data or selected portions of the data

block **1** a unit of storage consisting of one or more contiguous words, bytes, or logical records treated as a unit for reading or writing: typically, one block is read or written when a read or write command is issued. Blocked records reduce the amount of storage space needed for a file by decreasing the number of INTERRECORD GAPS. They also save input/output time by transmitting a group of data items as a unit **2** to so group words, bytes, or records

block diagram a diagram that uses symbols to describe the interconnections and flow of data between hardware and software components of a computer system. The symbols are simple geometric figures, such as rectangles or circles, that are connected by lines and arrows to indicate the operational direction of control or the flow of data between components: block diagrams are used to show the overall flow of a system Compare FLOWCHART, LOGIC DIAGRAM

block gap INTERRECORD GAP

blocking the process of grouping a specified number of logical records into a BLOCK Compare DEBLOCKING

blocking factor the number of LOGICAL RECORDS that form a block: a blocking factor is selected

by the programmer at the time the file is to be
stored on an external storage device. The selection is based upon the size of each logical record
and the type of hardware to be used for storage

block length BLOCK SIZE

block size a measure of the length of a block:
block size is usually expressed by the number of
bytes (or characters) per block

block sort a sorting technique that separates a
file into segments, orders each segment individually, and then rejoins the segments

block structure a programming technique in
which a program is constructed by grouping sequences of instructions into hierarchical blocks:
a block structure is a conceptual tool used to
create programs that are easy to follow and understand

BNF abbreviation for BACKUS–NAUR FORM

bomb to produce erroneous results or be unable
to execute because of incorrectly written logic
or syntax: primarily said of a program

bookkeeping HOUSEKEEPING

Boolean algebra an algebra defining the rules for
manipulating variables in symbolic logic: Boolean
algebra was developed as a method for express-
ing logical concepts in a mathematical form and
uses such logical operators as AND, OR, NOR, and
IF–THEN. It was developed by George Boole in
1847 and has since been applied to the designing of circuits in the computer

Boolean function an expression in Boolean algebra combining variables that can assume a value
of true or false (binary 1 or 0) with the various
LOGICAL OPERATORS: these functions are used in
designing circuits in a computer by defining the
output from various inputs

boot to bootstrap a routine, especially the operating system of a computer, into main memory

bootstrap 1 to enter several instructions of a routine into main memory in order to bring in the whole routine from an external storage device: the operating system of a computer can be bootstrapped into main memory by manually entering a few instructions or by hitting switches that initiate the execution of a few permanently stored instructions that load the operating system **2** referring to a technique for loading a routine into main memory by loading several instructions that bring the entire routine into main memory

bootstrap loader a hardware device in the computer that stores instructions for loading and transferring control to a routine whose first instructions are used to call the rest of the routine into main memory

BOP abbreviation for BIT–ORIENTED PROTOCOL

bounds register a nonaddressable register holding the upper and lower address bounds that a program is permitted to reference. Once an EFFECTIVE ADDRESS has been calculated, it is compared to the contents of the bounds register. If it is within the upper and lower bounds, a read or write operation is permitted; otherwise, an interrupt occurs. The bounds register prevents one program from interfering with another in a multiprogramming environment

BPAM (BEE pam) acronym for BASIC PARTITIONED ACCESS METHOD

bpi abbreviation for BITS PER INCH a measurement of the number of bits recorded per inch of recording surface

BPI abbreviation for BYTES PER INCH a measurement of the number of bytes recorded per inch of recording surface

bps abbreviation for BITS PER SECOND a measurement of the number of bits transmitted per second

branch **1** to transfer control to an instruction in a program other than the next sequential instruction **2** BRANCH INSTRUCTION See CONDITIONAL BRANCH, UNCONDITIONAL BRANCH

branch instruction an instruction in a program that causes the computer to branch to another instruction: instructions are executed in a regular sequence unless a branch instruction is introduced. Branch instructions give the programmer the ability to have different sets of instructions executed based on certain conditions. For example, a payroll program would have one set of instructions to control the calculation of payrate of salaried employees and a different set for calculating payrate of nonsalaried employees. Branch instructions allow each set of instructions to be executed only for appropriate records See UNCONDITIONAL BRANCH, CONDITIONAL BRANCH

breadboard **1** a board on which developing or experimental electronic circuits can be laid out: so called from the times when radios were constructed at home on a breadboard **2** to so construct a circuit

breakpoint the location in a program where normal execution is interrupted to allow for manual or software intervention. Breakpoints are usually used to DEBUG: for example, a programmer may insert an instruction to call for a dump at a strategic location in a program. This location would be called a breakpoint

broadband channel in data communications, a channel with a relatively large bandwidth that can transmit data at approximately 10,000 to 50,000 bits per second to and from higher-speed devices such as disk and tape drives, local terminals, and printers Compare VOICE–GRADE CHANNEL, NARROWBAND CHANNEL

broadband exchange a service offered by Western Union providing data communications over channels of a customer–selected bandwidth

BSAM (BEE sam) acronym for BASIC SEQUENTIAL ACCESS METHOD

BSC abbreviation for BINARY SYNCHRONOUS COMMUNICATION See BISYNC

BTAM (BEE tam) acronym for BASIC TELECOMMUNICATIONS ACCESS METHOD

bubble memory a solid–state memory device involving microscopic, magnetized areas, called "bubbles," in thin films of magnetic material, such as garnet. Initially, the bubbles are lined up in the same direction until a signal passes through the material causing certain bubbles to flip over. This negative or positive condition stores data according to the binary number system. Bubble memory is capable of storing very large amounts of data in very small space and has very fast access time. The memory is retained even when the input power is removed

bubble sort a sort in which each adjacent pair of items in the group to be sorted is compared: if they are not in the prescribed order, such as ascending, they exchange positions. This process is performed repeatedly on the entire list until no exchanges occur. The smallest item appears to bubble to the top

buffer an area of storage used to temporarily hold data being transferred from one device to another. A buffer is used to compensate for the different rates at which hardware devices process data: for example, a buffer would be used to hold data waiting to print, in order to free the CPU for other tasks, since it processes data at a much faster rate

buffer pool a number of buffers that are made available to the INPUT/OUTPUT CONTROL SYSTEM. Each buffer typically receives one physical record. When the record has been transmitted from the buffer, the buffer is returned to the pool

buffer storage **1** an EXTERNAL STORAGE device used as a buffer **2** BUFFER

bug **1** an error or mistake in a program **2** any hardware malfunction in a computer system

built–in check AUTOMATIC CHECK

bulk storage MASS STORAGE

bundled designating program packages and services that are sold together with a computer and its basic systems software Compare UNBUNDLED

burn–in a phase in the testing of components during which circuits are run for a specified length of time (usually one week) at a relatively high temperature in order to detect flaws

burst **1** in data communications, an unbroken stream of bits See BURST MODE **2** to separate continuous forms from one another

burster see CONTINUOUS FORMS

burst mode a communications mode in which a continuous block of data is transferred between main memory and an input/output device without interruption until the transfer has been completed Compare BYTE MODE

bus a circuit for the transfer of data or electrical signals between two devices

bus driver a device that amplifies the signal being transmitted on a bus

business data processing ADMINISTRATIVE DATA PROCESSING

byte a group of consecutive bits forming a unit of storage in the computer and used to represent one alphanumeric character: a byte usually consists of 8 bits but may contain more or fewer bits depending on the model of computer

byte–addressable designating a computer in which each byte has a unique address that can be used to access data in a program, as opposed to one in which only words have unique addresses Compare WORD–ADDRESSABLE

byte count oriented protocol a PROTOCOL that uses a special character to indicate the beginning of a MESSAGE containing a count of the number of data characters as well as the actual data. Once the data is transmitted, special characters follow to verify that the correct number of data characters has been sent

byte mode a communications mode in which bytes being transmitted by one device are interleaved with bytes being transmitted by another device Compare BURST MODE

bytewide memory a BYTE–ADDRESSABLE main memory

C

C in the HEXADECIMAL NUMBER SYSTEM, the symbol that corresponds to the decimal number 12

CA abbreviation for CONNECTING ARRANGEMENT

cable a bundle of insulated wires through which an electric current can be passed

cache memory a high–speed memory used as a buffer between the CPU and main memory: cache memory is used to store sequences of instructions from main memory. When the CPU needs an instruction, it first searches cache memory instead of the slower main memory. If the instruction is found in cache memory, it is called a **hit**. The ratio of the number of hits to the number of misses can be used to judge the effectiveness of the algorithms controlling the operation of cache memory

CAD acronym for COMPUTER–AIDED DESIGN

CAD/CAM acronym for COMPUTER–AIDED DESIGN/COMPUTER–AIDED MANUFACTURING a computer system used in engineering for such projects as designing parts and machinery, precisely calculating parts specifications, and generating complex wiring diagrams

CAI abbreviation for COMPUTER–ASSISTED INSTRUCTION

calculating machine CALCULATOR

calculating punch a device that performs arithmetic operations on data stored on a punch card and punches the result on the same card or another immediately following it

calculator a mechanical or electronic machine used for performing arithmetic operations: manual intervention is usually required to initiate each operation or series of operations. Prior to 1964, calculators were mechanical; the introduction of electronics eliminated moving parts, reduced noise, increased speed, and greatly reduced the size of the calculators

call 1 in a program, an instruction that transfers control to a routine, subroutine, or system program **2** to so transfer control See SUBROUTINE CALL, MACRO, SUPERVISOR CALL

calling program MAIN PROGRAM

calling sequence a sequence of assembly or machine language instructions that perform the transfer of control to a program, routine, or subroutine and return control back to the original program

CAM abbreviation for **1** COMPUTER-AIDED MANUFACTURING **2** CONTENT-ADDRESSABLE MEMORY

canned routine a prewritten program, sold for use with a particular computer, that performs one or more generalized functions, such as sorting, standard mathematical calculations, or payroll

capacity the amount of information that all or part of a computer system, such as main memory or a disk pack, can store: for example, the capacity of a computer's main memory could be 512K of information (524,288 characters)

card 1 PUNCH CARD **2** a printed circuit board inserted into a computer to provide additional memory

card code the combinations of punched holes that represent numbers, letters, and special characters in a PUNCH CARD See HOLLERITH CODE

card column any of the vertical lines on a PUNCH CARD where holes can be punched

card deck a group of punched cards forming a program and/or a data file

card feed a mechanism on a unit record device, such as a keypunch or card reader, that removes a PUNCH CARD from the CARD HOPPER and places it in position for processing

card field a number of columns on a PUNCH CARD used to store one field of a record

card hopper a part of a unit record device, such as a keypunch or card reader, used to hold PUNCH CARDS that are ready to be processed Compare CARD STACKER

card image **1** the representation of data on a terminal, a printed page, or a disk in the standard columns found on a punch card **2** the representation of a punched card in which the pattern of punched and unpunched positions is represented as a matrix of 1's and 0's

card punch a device attached to a computer, that is used to produce output in the form of PUNCH CARDS: a card punch might be used for making a BACKUP COPY of a program or data

card random access memory (or method) CRAM

card reader a device that reads the data stored on a PUNCH CARD into the computer: the punch card can be passed over a photoelectric device that senses the holes or it can be passed over reading brushes that make electrical contact with a metal roller when a hole is encountered. A card hopper holds the card deck being read. Each card is automatically fed into the reader, passed over the reading mechanism, and then placed in the card stacker behind the last card read. A card reader may also incorporate other mechanisms to sort, collate, punch, or interpret cards

card reproducer REPRODUCING PUNCH

card row any of the horizontal lines on a PUNCH CARD where holes can be punched

card sorter an earlier device used to sort PUNCH CARDS mechanically

card stacker a part of a unit record device, such as a keypunch or card reader, that receives and holds PUNCH CARDS after they have been processed Compare CARD HOPPER

card–to–disk (or tape) converter a program that copies the data stored on a punch card onto disk (or tape)

card verification KEY VERIFICATION

carriage a device that moves CONTINUOUS FORMS through a printer

carriage control tape a strip of punched paper or plastic tape used to control the carriage of a printer

carriage return **1** a key on some terminals used as an ENTER KEY or to return to the first position on the next line **2** a device on a printer that returns the print mechanism to the first print position on a page

carrier a signal of continuous frequency that is supplied by a public utility, such as a telephone or telegraph company, along a communication line: this frequency can then be modulated by a device such as a MODEM in order to transmit data from one location to another

carrier detect a pin on an interface for a modem that indicates whether the receiver section of the modem is or is not receiving transmitted data: one of the standards used by RS–232–C and CCITT V.24

carry the digit that is to be added in the next higher position when two digits are added and the sum exceeds one digit position: for example, the addition of 5 plus 6 results in a carry of 1 to the next digit position and the addition of binary

1 plus 1 results in a carry of 1 to the next bit position

cartridge a protective container that is used for the storage of a reel of magnetic tape and that may include a take–up reel

cascaded carry in a PARALLEL COMPUTER, the process of adding the carries into the sum and, if any additional carries result, adding them into the sum, and so on until no further carries result

cassette a small cartridge containing a reel of magnetic tape and a take–up reel, most commonly used in microcomputer systems

catalog 1 a table that contains descriptive information for each data set stored in the computer system **2** to so enter information into a table

cataloged data set a data set whose name has been entered into a catalog along with other descriptive information

cataloged procedure PROCEDURE (sense 3)

catenate clipped form of CONCATENATE

cathode ray tube CRT

CCITT abbreviation for COMITÉ CONSULTATIF INTERNATIONAL TÉLÉPHONIQUE et TÉLÉGRAPHIQUE an international committee providing standards for data communication between countries

CCITT V.24 in data communications, a set of standards specifying the characteristics for interfaces, including descriptions of the various functions provided by each of the pins: similar in structure to RS–232–C

CE abbreviation for CHIP ENABLE

cell 1 STORAGE LOCATION **2** MEMORY CELL **3** a unit of storage capable of holding one byte or one character **4** the unit of storage that holds one record

centisecond one–hundredth of a second

centralized data processing DATA PROCESSING in an organization that is performed at one, central location. The data may be obtained from all areas within the organization, including field office operations Compare DECENTRALIZED DATA PROCESSING

central processing unit CPU

central processor CPU

chad the chip of paper removed when a hole is punched in a paper tape or a PUNCH CARD

chain a group of logically related items linked together by a POINTER contained in each item

chained file a file in which all the records that share a common key are linked (or chained) together by a pointer contained in each record: chained files usually have directories that contain the address of the first record in a chain. They provide faster access than sequential files but require more storage space for the pointers and directory

chaining a programming technique in which records or fields are stored with logically related data by including a pointer in each item to the next member in the group. The data need not be stored in consecutive storage locations since the pointers provide the link between the data See CHAINED FILE, LINKED LIST

chaining search a search technique in which an item in a chain is found by following the pointers from item to item until the desired one is located or the end of the chain is reached

chain printer an IMPACT PRINTER that prints a line of FULLY FORMED CHARACTERS by striking individual embossed characters on a continuously rotating metal band or chain against an inked ribbon and paper, one line at a time: the chain is composed of 48 different characters that are arranged in five, 48–character sections for faster printing

channel   **1** a row for the recording of data on a paper or magnetic tape or on a magnetic card **2** COMMUNICATION CHANNEL **3** clipped form of INPUT/OUTPUT CHANNEL **4** a column in which a hole may be punched on a CARRIAGE CONTROL TAPE

channel–attached LOCAL

channel capacity   the maximum rate at which a channel can transmit data: channel capacity is usually expressed in bits, bytes, or kilobytes per second and can be affected by the way data is stored (if the data is not in contiguous storage locations, the rate is slower), by the way a channel is programmed, by the operation of other channels, or by the CPU (the CPU and the channel may use the same registers, for example)

channel command an instruction that is executed by an input/output channel: it usually consists of the operation to be performed, such as a read or write, the address of where the data is stored, and a count of the data items to be read or written. The entire set of commands is called a **channel program** and consists of a number of instructions for each type of input/output device connected to the channel

character   an alphabetic letter, digit, or special symbol

character–addressable BYTE–ADDRESSABLE

character code a code that represents characters as specific bit patterns

character density DENSITY (sense 1)

character fill a character, such as a blank or other nondata character, placed into a storage location in order to replace unwanted data: for example, if a storage location is first used to hold the value "ABCDE" and is then replaced with the value " FG", the blanks have been used as character fill for the first three positions

characteristic **1** the exponent of a number in FLOATING–POINT NOTATION **2** the integer number, which may be positive or negative, in the representation of a logarithm: for example, in the representation of $LOG_{10}0.0402 = -1.3958$, -1 is the characteristic and .3958 is the MANTISSA

character–oriented protocol a PROTOCOL that uses special characters to indicate the beginning of a MESSAGE and the end of a block of data: IBM's binary synchronous protocol, called BISYNC, is an example of character–oriented protocol

character printer a printer that prints only one character at a time See DAISY–WHEEL PRINTER, ELECTROSTATIC PRINTER, INK–JET PRINTER, THERMAL PRINTER, THIMBLE PRINTER, WIRE–MATRIX PRINTER Compare PAGE PRINTER, LINE PRINTER

character set the set of characters that may be used in a given computer or programming language: character sets differ in the number of characters, the specific characters allowed, and their collating sequence

character string a sequence of characters, numbers, and/or special symbols used as a constant or variable in a program: the string is usually enclosed in apostrophes or quotation marks to define it within the program

check a process that determines the accuracy of data, such as a PARITY CHECK, CYCLIC REDUNDANCY CHECK, or OVERFLOW CHECK

check bit a bit added to a unit of data, such as a byte or a word, that is used in performing a check

check character a character appended to a unit of data, such as a block, that is used in performing a check

check digit a digit appended to a number to insure the accuracy of the number when it is read or written: the digit is formed by performing a calculation on the number. Each time the number is read or written, the same calculation is performed, and the new check digit is compared to the original. If digits in the number have been transposed, omitted, or repeated, the new check digit will be different from the original and the error is thus detected

check indicator **1** in a register, a bit set to a value of 1 or 0 to indicate that an error condition has or has not occurred **2** a light or sound on a device that is activated when an error or malfunction has occurred during its operation

checkpoint **1** a designated place in a program where normal execution is interrupted and data concerning the status of the program, such as the contents of registers and the storage locations used by the program, are stored temporarily on an external storage device. A checkpoint is used to avoid the repeated execution of the entire program if an error or malfunction should occur. If one does occur, it can be corrected and execution of the program can be resumed from the last checkpoint **2** to so preserve information about a program **3** referring to information so preserved

checkpoint restart the process of resuming the execution of a program from the last checkpoint. It is performed by a routine that reads in and restores the checkpoint information from an external storage device

Chinese binary COLUMN–BINARY

chip an INTEGRATED CIRCUIT created on a tiny silicon flake upon which a large number of gates and the paths connecting them are formed by very thin films of metal acting as wires: the chip can be used as main memory or as a CPU. When both memory and logic capabilities are contained in the same chip, it is called a **microprocessor** or a **computer on a chip**. The chip consumes very little power, is compact and of low cost, and can currently process as many as a million or more instructions per second. The chip is used in a wide, ever–increasing variety of devices such as personal computers, calculators, digital watches, robots, and electronic games

chip enable CHIP SELECT

chip select a pin on a chip used to enable or disable the reading or writing of data from or onto the chip

circuit **1** an arrangement of electrical elements through which electric current flows **2** in data communications, a line composed of a channel for sending data and one for receiving data

circuit switching in data communications, a technique in which an electrical connection is made between the sending and receiving locations and is held until the entire transmission of data is made: this is called circuit switching because the computer or software used to establish the electrical connection is capable of switching the connection between a number of

sending and receiving terminals or computers
Compare PACKET SWITCHING, MESSAGE SWITCHING

circular list a LINKED LIST in which the last item in
the list includes a pointer to the first item in the
list

circular shift a SHIFT in which the bit or bits from
one end of a register are shifted into the opposite end of the same register: there is no loss of
bits in a circular shift Compare LOGICAL SHIFT

clear **1** to change the contents of a memory location to zero **2** to cancel the contents of a register in a calculator **3** to erase displayed characters from the screen of a CRT

clear to send a pin on an interface for a modem
indicating whether the modem is ready to accept data, from a terminal or computer, for transmission: one of the standards used by RS-232-C.
In CCITT V.24 the corresponding pin is called
ready for sending

CLK abbreviation for CLOCK

clock in synchronous computers, a circuit that
sends out signals at precise frequencies to
schedule the operation of the computer: each
operation takes a specified number of signals,
and the CONTROL UNIT can then initiate the
proper operations at correct intervals

clock time CYCLE TIME

close in a program, to terminate access to a file
Compare OPEN

closed loop in PROCESS CONTROL, the type of system in which a computer can respond to feedback from a sensor or control equipment without
intervention from a human operator: for example, the computer could adjust the temperature in a furnace Compare OPEN LOOP

closed shop the operating policy of a computer system in which only the professional staff is permitted to operate the computer and its peripheral equipment: most large computer centers are closed shops due to the cost and complexity of operating the equipment and to insure the security of data and equipment

closed subroutine a subroutine that is written only once but is called from a number of different locations in a program: a closed subroutine has statements at the beginning to handle the variables coming into it from the main program and statements at the end to transfer the results and control back to the main program. This implementation of a subroutine is referred to as **out–of–line coding** Compare OPEN SUBROUTINE

cluster a group of terminals connected to a CONTROLLER

CM abbreviation for CORRECTIVE MAINTENANCE

coax clipped form of COAXIAL CABLE

coaxial cable a cable used for the transmission of data in a communication system: coaxial cable is capable of carrying more messages at higher rates of speed than conventional telephone lines

COBOL acronym for **CO**MMON **B**USINESS **O**RIENTED **L**ANGUAGE a high–level programming language capable of performing all the necessary calculations most often used in business: it is specifically designed to handle highly structured records stored in a wide variety of data structures and storage devices. COBOL is the primary language used in administrative data processing since its use of English terms makes programs easy to read, modify, and maintain

CODASYL (KOH dah sill) acronym for **CON-FERENCE ON DATA SYSTEMS LANGUAGES** a volunteer organization of persons in the computer and data processing industries, formed in 1958, to help standardize programming languages for easier transfer among different types of computers

code **1** a set of rules defining the way in which bits can be arranged to represent numbers, letters, and special symbols: each computer uses a type of code, such as ASCII or EBCDIC **2** to assign meanings to a set of numbers, letters, or special symbols **3** to write a program **4** one or more instructions in a program **5** to assign a character to represent a larger item of data so that less storage space is used, as in assigning the number **1** to mean college graduate, **2** for high school graduate, and so on

codec (KOH dek) acronym for **CODER/DECODER** an integrated circuit for digital–to–analog and analog–to–digital conversion in a PCM system

coder **1** a programmer who writes programs designed by other, usually more experienced, programmers or systems analysts **2** ENCODER

coder/decoder CODEC

coding form a form marked with rows and columns on which a program is written: coding forms are usually provided for the more commonly used programming languages, such as COBOL and FORTRAN, and are shaded in various colors and marked to assist in the proper positioning of programming statements as required by the particular language

cold start the IPL of a computer in which jobs waiting to print and to execute and various other data concerning the system are erased when the computer is shut down: for example, a cold start may be needed when loading a new version of an OPERATING SYSTEM Compare WARM START

collate to combine two ordered files into one file in the same sequence

collating sequence the ordering sequence assigned to the characters in a computer so that data items can be ordered: characters are arranged in the order of their internal numerical representation with letters arranged in alphabetical order and numbers and special symbols arranged according to the particular code: for example, in ASCII, numbers have a lower value than letters, whereas in EBCDIC, they have a higher value

collator a machine that collates punched cards and may also perform various other functions, such as selecting those cards containing an error in specified fields, checking the sequence of cards, and matching cards that belong to a selected group or groups

collision the occurrence of two or more record keys that have been converted to the same hash address See HASHING

column CARD COLUMN

column–binary designating the representation of a binary number in each column of a punch card: for example, a 12–bit binary number could be represented in one column of a 12–row punch card Compare ROW–BINARY

COM (KAHM) acronym for **C**OMPUTER **O**UTPUT **M**ICROFILM or **M**ICROFILMING a printer or the technique for recording computer output on microfilm

comb a device that supports the access arms on a disk drive: the access arms are supported in a single column and appear much like the teeth on a comb

combinational circuit an arrangement of inter-connected gates that form a circuit to perform various logical operations in the computer: combinational circuits are used in half–adders, full–adders, decoders, and other such devices that do not require the capability of storing bits: for example, a full–adder adds two incoming bits and outputs the sum Compare SEQUENTIAL CIRCUIT

command 1 a request entered on a terminal to have a function performed: for example, a print command would cause the contents of a file to be printed on the terminal **2** clipped form of CHANNEL COMMAND **3** loosely, INSTRUCTION

command language 1 a language used on a terminal to create, store, and modify programs and/or data **2** JCL

command mode a mode of operation for a terminal in which various commands can be entered as needed to place the terminal in EDIT MODE or INPUT MODE, or to perform various other functions, such as storing a file

comments optional, descriptive remarks that explain the various steps and techniques used, added to a program in order to make the program easier to understand or alter: comments are not executed but are printed in the program listing

common area an area of main memory used to store data that will be used by several OVERLAY SEGMENTS of the same program

common business oriented language COBOL

common carrier in data communications, a public or private telephone, telegraph, or other telecommunication company that is licensed by the FTC to provide services for the purpose of data transmission

common language a programming language, such as COBOL or FORTRAN, that can be used on a variety of different computers

common program a program that solves a commonly encountered problem, such as finding the square root of a number, and is most commonly stored in a library where it can be called into use by a wide variety of programs

communication the process of transferring data from one device to another in a computer system, as from a terminal to the computer

communication channel a path for the transmission of data

communication interface INTERFACE (sense 1)

communication line 1 a line for the transmission of data, as a telephone line or coaxial cable 2 COMMUNICATION CHANNEL

communication link the hardware and software providing the means by which two devices, such as a computer and a terminal, are connected for transmitting data

communication protocol PROTOCOL

communications control character a control character used to provide information about data being transmitted or to control its transmission, such as an END OF TRANSMISSION character

communications controller a device that gathers and routes all data being transmitted between a computer and various terminals in the computer system

communications processor COMMUNICATIONS CONTROLLER

communications satellite a man–made satellite in orbit around the earth that relays microwave transmission, as between computer locations separated by great distances

communications terminal TERMINAL

companding contraction of **COM**PRESSING EX-**PANDING** the process of recoding bits into a more compact form for transmission, and recovering the original form at the receiving end

comparator **1** a circuit that compares two signals and indicates whether they are the same, as both binary 1 or 0 **2** a device that compares two transcriptions of the same data as a check on accuracy and notes any discrepancies between the two

compare to determine the relationship between two items of data, such as whether one is greater than, less than, or equal to, the other

comparison a logical operation in which a data item is established to be greater than, less than, or equal to another data item: a further action is usually taken depending on the result of the comparison: for example, "IF A>B THEN C=0" is a programming statement in which the comparison of A and B determine whether C will equal zero

comparison operator RELATIONAL OPERATOR

compatible **1** designating two computers or software systems, such as language processors, that produce identical results when a program is transferred from one to the other **2** designating computer components and peripheral equipment that can be used with a specific computer system

compilation the process performed by a compiler

compile–and–go the process of compiling a program and then loading the OBJECT PROGRAM into main memory for execution: a compiler that can perform this function is called a **load–and–go compiler** and is frequently used when a batch of source programs written in the same source language are compiled and executed one at a time. The load–and–go compiler can remain in memory until the entire batch has been executed instead of being loaded into memory each time a new source program is to be compiled

compiler a program that translates a source program written in a high–level language into its equivalent machine language: the compiler may translate the source program into an assembly language program, in which case the compiler has an assembler to further translate the program into machine language. The output program from a compiler is called an OBJECT PROGRAM. A compiler also produces a program listing and diagnostics that result from errors detected in the translating process Compare INTERPRETER (sense 1)

compiler–compiler a program that produces a compiler as output

compiler language a high–level language requiring a compiler to translate it into machine language

compiler program COMPILER

complement the number denoting the difference between a specified number and the next higher power of its base See ONE'S COMPLEMENT, TWO'S COMPLEMENT, TEN'S COMPLEMENT

complement form the representation of the negative of a number as the complement of the number: a negative number is usually stored in

memory in complement form See TWO'S COMPLE-
MENT Compare TRUE FORM

complex number any number of the form **a + bi**,
where **a** and **b** are real numbers and **i** is the
square root of –1; **i** is called the **imaginary unit**,
a is called the **real part**, and the real coefficient
b is called the **imaginary part**

component any of the units or devices that com-
prise a computer system, such as a disk, tape
drive, or CPU, and perform given functions

compute–bound designating a computer system
or program that is performing more computations than INPUT/OUTPUT OPERATIONS Compare
I/O–BOUND, BALANCED SYSTEM

computer an electronic device for performing
high–speed arithmetic and logical operations,
composed of five basic components—an ALU,
control unit, input and output devices, and
memory: data is received, transmitted, stored,
processed, and output with minimal human intervention. The three general classifications of computers are the MICROCOMPUTER, MINICOMPUTER,
and MAINFRAME, whose differences depend on
the type of processor, size of memory, and
input/output devices used. Because of rapid advances in technology, the boundaries between
these classifications are not clearly defined See
ANALOG COMPUTER, DIGITAL COMPUTER

computer–aided design the use of a computer to
design a device or a system, display it on a CRT
or as a printout, simulate its operation, and provide statistics on its performance. The computer
is provided with data concerning the item to be
designed, how it is to function, and the rules for
the way in which the different components can
be joined

computer–aided manufacturing manufacturing that is assisted by the use of computers and NUMERICAL CONTROL devices

computer–assisted instruction the use of a computer to provide educational exercises, such as drills, practice sessions, and tutorial lessons, for a student: a terminal is used to respond to exercises that have been programmed to assist students at their individual level of ability and speed of learning

computer center an office that provides computer services, such as the operation of a computer and the peripheral equipment, the writing of application programs and computer reports, and various other services to a wide variety of people: the computer center may operate as an OPEN SHOP or as a CLOSED SHOP

computer code MACHINE CODE

computerese the specialized vocabulary and idioms used in computer terminology: a somewhat derogatory term implying some unintelligibility

computer family all the models, collectively, of a single type of computer, sharing the same logical design

computer generations the various stages in the development of digital computers See FIRST GENERATION COMPUTER, SECOND GENERATION COMPUTER, THIRD GENERATION COMPUTER, FOURTH GENERATION COMPUTER

computer graphics the use of a computer to produce pictorial representations of relationships, such as charts, and two– or three-dimensional images, by means of dots, lines, curves, etc: the data can be entered through various devices in the form of lines or drawings or can be entered through a keyboard. Once the image has been produced on a screen, it may be manipulated by moving, rotating, or elongating it with devices such as a light pen or track ball

computer instruction MACHINE INSTRUCTION

computer instruction set MACHINE INSTRUCTION SET

computerize 1 to equip an industry, office, or the like with computers so as to facilitate or automate procedures **2** to convert a manual operation into one that is performed by a computer

computer language MACHINE LANGUAGE

computer logic the way in which the various logic devices and functional units in a computer are combined to determine the various logical operations of which a computer is capable

computer–managed instruction the use of a computer to assist an instructor with the details involved in monitoring the progress of students: for example, the computer is used to print and grade tests, to store the results and print reports based on them, and to produce statistics that guide the instructor in determining areas that need to be stressed or reviewed

computer operation MACHINE OPERATION

computer operator a person who performs the manual activities needed for the efficient operation of a computer system: computer operators mount tapes on drives, mount and align the proper paper on printers, respond to messages from the computer, maintain logs, monitor the activity in the computer system, detect and often resolve errors in equipment, and the like

computer–oriented language MACHINE–ORIENTED LANGUAGE

computer output microfilm COM

computer program PROGRAM

computer science the field concerned with the design and application of computer hardware and software

computer system a system composed of a computer (or computers), peripheral equipment, such as disks, printers, and terminals, and the software necessary to make them operate together

computer utility a computer center that supplies computing services to the general public for a fee through the use of terminals, much in the same way that water and electricity are supplied by public utilities

computer word WORD

computing the process of performing operations on data in order to obtain a desired result

concatenate to join two or more items, such as character strings or files, end to end to form a larger unit: for example, two files can be concatenated by appending all the records in one file to the end of the records in another file. This larger file is said to be a **concatenated data set**

concatenation operator a symbol in a programming language that is used to join two CHARACTER STRINGS: the concatenation operator is usually two vertical bars $|$: for example, if A is a character string equaling "WHY", and B equals "NOT", then A $|$ B equals "WHYNOT"

concentrator a processor that is programmed to combine transmitted data from several low-speed devices, such as terminals, into data that is then transmitted over one line at a much higher speed and usually to a distant CPU: it can also be programmed to perform other functions such as polling and detecting errors

concordance a list of the principal words and phrases appearing in a document, arranged alphabetically with references to passages in which they occur or with the actual context of each occurrence: the computer can be used to create, update, and maintain such a list

concurrent execution the execution of two or more programs that are in main memory within the same period: each is executed for a designated interval

concurrent operation the performance of two or more operations within a given time interval, thus forming the basis for TIMESHARING Compare SIMULTANEOUS PROCESSING

condition an occurrence during the execution of a program about which data is recorded and subsequently used to determine further action: for example, when OVERFLOW occurs, a bit is set to indicate that it has happened, causing an interrupt

conditional branch a branch instruction in which a condition is tested to determine whether the branch will occur: for example, a payroll program could include a conditional branch that tested whether or not an employee had taken sick time. If not, the program would branch to an instruction following those that subtracted the number of sick hours from the employee's accumulated allowance. If sick time was taken, the branch would not occur Compare UNCONDITIONAL BRANCH

conditional operator a logical operator used in a conditional statement, such as IF–THEN or IF–THEN–ELSE

conditional statement in a program, a statement in which a condition is tested to determine whether or not a further action will occur: for example, "If A=1 THEN B=2" is a conditional state-

ment in which the further action of having B
equal 2 will be taken only when A equals 1

conditional transfer CONDITIONAL BRANCH

condition code a code used to identify a certain
condition that occurs during the execution of a
program and that is subsequently tested to determine further activity: for example, a condition
code is often used to identify whether the result
of an arithmetic operation, such as an add or
subtract, is negative, positive, or zero. If the condition code indicates a negative result after the
addition of two positive numbers, an error is
detected and the program may terminate execution or may branch to a subroutine to handle the
error

conditioning improvements made to a leased line
in order to reduce the amount of interference
and attenuation occurring during the transmission of data

configuration the way in which a computer (or
computers) and peripheral equipment are interconnected and programmed to operate as a system

conjunction an AND operation

connecting arrangement an electrical interface
device required by telephone companies when
customer-owned terminals and their related
equipment are connected to leased private lines
of the telephone network Compare DATA ACCESS
ARRANGEMENT

connect time the amount of time a terminal is
connected to the computer, measured from the
time of LOG ON until the time of LOG OFF

consecutive designating successive events or
storage locations, with no intervening event or
location

console **1** OPERATOR CONSOLE **2** loosely, TERMINAL

constant a value that remains unchanged during the execution of a program: for example, in a payroll program, the rate of pay for a certain type of employee would be a constant

constraint in MATHEMATICAL PROGRAMMING, any of the equations or inequalities specified in a problem that create restrictions which limit the solution to the optimal one

content all the addressable data in a particular storage location of main memory

content–addressable memory ASSOCIATIVE MEMORY

contention the condition when two or more devices or programs request the same resource, such as a tape drive: if only one is available, the contention may be resolved on a first come, first served basis or by assigning a priority to one of the programs or devices

contiguous designating adjacent storage locations in main memory or auxiliary storage

continuation card (or **line**) a punch card (or line on a screen of a CRT) containing the portion of a programming statement that was too long to fit on the previous card (or line)

continuous data data that can assume an indefinite number of values, as in recording temperature Compare DISCRETE DATA

continuous error an error that occurs repeatedly and requires manual intervention or correction to restore normal functioning Compare INTERMITTENT ERROR

continuous forms forms fed into a printer on a continuous roll with perforations at regular intervals: after printing, the forms can be separated at the perforations by a machine called a burster. If the forms have carbon copies, the carbon paper can be removed and the copies separated by a machine called a **decollator**

continuous processing the processing of data, as it occurs, on a continuous basis: for example, in PROCESS CONTROL, a computer may be used to continuously monitor the temperature in a furnace in order to determine when adjustments should be made Compare BATCH PROCESSING

control the process carried out by a control unit

control break **1** a program that is used to print out various items of intermediate information, such as subtotals and headings, when a change occurs in a field, as from one department number to another **2** such a change in a field

control bus a path along which control signals are transmitted See SYSTEM BUS

control cards **1** those statements in a program that contain JCL: control cards usually precede the source program to identify the programmer, the language processor needed, the data files needed, and to signal the beginning of the source statements. There are also control cards to signal the end of the program to the computer **2** loosely, programming statements used in a software package, such as SPSS

control character a character that is embedded in a data item to specify an operation to be performed: for example, a line to be printed could contain a control character indicating that the printer should advance two lines before printing on the page

control counter PROGRAM COUNTER

control field a field in a record indicating the meaning that is to be given to a previous or subsequent field in the record: for example, it could indicate, when its value is one, that the next five numbers represent an amount to be subtracted from a checking account, and when its value is zero, that it is an amount to be added to the account

control function any function to control the operation of equipment, such as the starting and stopping of the movement of tape over the read/write head of a tape drive

controlled variable a variable that assumes a given set of values determined by a program: for example, a loop often has a controlled variable that assumes a value based on the number of times the loop has executed. The program determines the values because it starts the value at a number and adds or subtracts 1 each time the loop executes

controller a device that controls the operation of another device or system, such as an I/O controller that controls the operation of an input/output device

control memory a memory in the CONTROL UNIT used to store microinstructions: it may be a ROM, a PROM, or a **writable control memory**, in which the microinstructions can be altered by a programmer

control panel **1** a panel that is part of an operator console containing various light indicators, switches, and buttons used to turn power on and off, to control components in the computer system, and to monitor activities in the computer **2** PLUGBOARD

control procedure DATA LINK CONTROL

control programs SYSTEM PROGRAMS that control the allocation of resources in a computer system, such as the printers, disks, main memory, and tape drives, so as to decrease the amount of human intervention in the system: the two main types of control programs are the SUPERVISOR and the JOB CONTROL PROGRAM

control punch a hole punched in a punch card to be used as a CONTROL FIELD or a CONTROL CHARACTER

control read–only memory CROM

control register a nonaddressable register storing control information used by the operating system and hardware

control section   **1** CONTROL UNIT   **2** part of a program that performs a specified function, such as reading the data from a magnetic tape, and that can be replaced or altered without affecting the rest of the program

control sequence the sequence in which instructions are executed in a program one at a time in order unless a branch instruction transfers the control

control signals electrical signals to and from the control unit that direct the sequence of operations to be performed by the computer

control statement an instruction that affects the sequence in which the instructions in a program are executed, such as a BRANCH INSTRUCTION

control unit   **1** an element in the CPU that receives an instruction from a program in main memory, decodes it, and sends signals to the appropriate units in the computer to execute the instruction: the control unit directs the operation of the computer as a whole   **2** CONTROLLER

control word a WORD containing descriptive information about a record or a block: for example, a control word might contain information about the length and the address of data that is to be transferred from main memory to a disk. The control word is used by a processor, in this case an INPUT/OUTPUT CHANNEL, in order to perform a function

conversational designating a method of using a terminal to control the execution of a program step–by–step, in which there is a response from the computer at each step that may be used in determining further steps

conversational language a programming language, such as BASIC, that closely resembles human language and is used on a terminal operating in conversational mode

conversational mode the mode of operation in which program statements or data are entered one line at a time on a terminal, and the computer immediately responds to each line by sending a message back to the terminal for the operator to view: this continuous exchange between the computer and the terminal operator is often called a **dialogue**

conversational programming programming in which each statement is typed into the terminal and executed: there is a continuous exchange of information between the computer and the programmer, in ordinary language, that allows changes and additions to be made during each step. The programmer is often prompted with requests that data be entered, inquiries as to whether the program should be stored or executed, and the like

conversational system a teleprocessing system that operates in a conversational mode

conversion 1 the process of changing procedures, methods, and programs to conform to the requirements of new or updated equipment and systems, as from the use of punched cards to the use of terminals as the primary means of entering programs and data into the computer **2** DATA CONVERSION

conversion table a table showing the various characters in one code and their corresponding representation in another, such as one showing the characters in the EBCDIC code and their binary and hexadecimal notations

core clipped form of CORE MEMORY

core dump DUMP (sense 1)

core memory a type of memory composed of storage units, called **magnetic cores,** made from a ferromagnetic material and magnetized in either of two directions to store a bit: core memory is the earliest type of memory used in computers. It is nonvolatile and has a destructive–read property requiring that data be restored after it has been read Compare SEMICONDUCTOR MEMORY, BUBBLE MEMORY

core storage CORE MEMORY

corrective maintenance a plan or service for isolating and correcting malfunctions in equipment after they occur See DIAGNOSTIC ROUTINE Compare PREVENTIVE MAINTENANCE

counter **1** a variable used in a program to keep track of the number of times an event has occurred: the counter is started at zero and increased by one each time an event occurs, or it is started at the number of times the event is supposd to occur and decreased by one each time until it reaches zero **2** a logic device used to count the number of times an event occurs in the circuitry of the computer See PROGRAM COUNTER

cpi abbreviation for CHARACTERS PER INCH

CPM abbreviation for CRITICAL PATH METHOD a technique for managing projects in which the various tasks to be completed are ordered and the length of time for their completion is determined: the sequence of activities with the longest completion time is called the **critical path** and establishes the shortest completion time for the entire project, if everything progresses as scheduled See PERT

cps abbreviation for **1** CHARACTERS PER SECOND **2** CYCLES PER SECOND See HERTZ

CPU abbreviaton for CENTRAL PROCESSING UNIT the portion of a computer composed of the ALU and the CONTROL UNIT: every computer has a CPU. It is where instructions are fetched, decoded, and executed, and the overall activity of the computer is controlled

CPU time the amount of time required to execute a set of instructions in the CPU: CPU time does not include the time spent waiting for input/output operations to be performed and, therefore, will differ from the time between the start and end of execution Compare REAL TIME

CR abbreviation for CARRIAGE RETURN

CRAM acronym for **C**ARD **R**ANDOM **A**CCESS **M**EMORY or **M**ETHOD **1** a trademark for a DIRECT ACCESS STORAGE DEVICE composed of removable cartridges, each of which contains several hundred magnetic cards that can be individually selected from the cartridge and wrapped around a rotating drum in order to access the stored data **2** a method for so accessing data

crash 1 an instance of becoming inoperable because of a malfunction in the equipment or an error in the program See also HEAD CRASH **2** to so become inoperable

CRC abbreviation for CYCLIC REDUNDANCY CHECK a check performed on a block of data to determine whether an error has occurred in the reading, writing, or transmission of data: a CRC is performed by reading a block of data, calculating the CRC CHARACTER, and comparing its value to the CRC character already present in the block. If they are equal, the data is assumed to be correct; otherwise, an error has been detected Compare LRC, VRC

CRC character a CHECK CHARACTER appended to a block of data: a CRC character is generated by treating a block of data as a serial string of bits that represent a binary number, dividing that number by another predetermined binary number, and appending the remainder from the division to the block of data as a CRC character

critical path method CPM

CROM acronym for **C**ONTROL **R**EAD–**O**NLY **M**EMORY a ROM used to store a microprogram permanently

cross assembler (or **compiler)** an ASSEMBLER (or COMPILER) used on one computer to translate programs that are to be executed on another, usually smaller, computer: cross assemblers (or compilers) are used to take advantage of the greater speed and memory available on the larger computer

cross–check to check a result by calculating it by two different methods

crossfoot check a test performed to determine the accuracy of a total sum, performed by calculating a sum through two different methods and then comparing the totals: if the totals do not match, an error has occurred in the program:

for example, gross pay should be equal to the sum of net pay, taxes, and deductions

cross–reference table a table produced by a language processor containing each variable and constant used in a program, its corresponding value, and those instructions in which it is used: often used in debugging or modifying a program since it quickly identifies where each variable or constant is used

CRT abbreviation for CATHODE RAY TUBE a screen like that of a television receiver, used in computer systems for viewing data: it typically displays 20 to 24 lines of data with 60 to 80 characters per line. A CRT may be used in place of a printer and, with an attached keyboard, forms a TERMINAL

cryogenics the study of the effects of very low temperatures (usually below $-420°$ F, or $-215°$ C) on the properties of matter: at such temperatures, certain metals, alloys, and other materials lose their electrical resistance, thereby greatly increasing their conductivity, and can be used with low power requirements for the high–speed storage of bits

CS abbreviation for CHIP SELECT

CTS abbreviation for CLEAR TO SEND

CU abbreviation for CONTROL UNIT

current address register PROGRAM COUNTER

current instruction the instruction that is being executed

current loop a serial transmission standard in which a pair of wires connecting the receiving and sending devices transmit binary 0 when no current flows, and a binary 1 when current is flowing

cursor a visual position indicator on a display terminal, such as a CRT, that moves along with each character as it is entered from the keyboard: it is most commonly a short, highlighted line that appears underneath the space where a character is to be entered or replaced

cybernetics the science dealing with the comparative study of complex electronic systems and animal, especially the human, nervous systems: the science was introduced in the 1940s by a group of engineers and scientists led primarily by Norbert Wiener and Arturo Rosenblueth

cycle a sequence of events that repeats itself in regular patterns until the operation is concluded, such as an INSTRUCTION CYCLE

cycles per second HERTZ

cycle stealing the use of a memory cycle by an INPUT/OUTPUT CHANNEL, during which time the CPU is unable to access main memory: the cycle is said to be stolen because the channel is given the memory cycle in preference to the CPU. During this time, the CPU must stop and wait for the next memory cycle. This is called **hesitation**, and the CPU is said to be **locked out** of main memory

cycle time the time that elapses from one successive read or write operation to another in main memory

cyclic redundancy check CRC

cyclic redundancy check character CRC CHARACTER

cyclic shift CIRCULAR SHIFT

cylinder any of the vertical columns of TRACKS that are one above another in a DISK PACK: if each disk contains 200 tracks, there will be 200 cylinders numbered in order in the disk pack. All the tracks with the same number form a cylinder. Data is stored in a cylinder, rather than in consecutively numbered tracks, since all the tracks of a single cylinder can be accessed by one movement of the ACCESS ARM, shortening the time needed to read or write data

D

D in the HEXADECIMAL NUMBER SYSTEM, the symbol that corresponds to the decimal number 13

DAA abbreviation for DATA ACCESS ARRANGEMENT

DAC abbreviation for DIGITAL–TO–ANALOG CONVERTER

daisy chain interrupt an interrupt system in which the peripheral devices are connected to the computer along a single bus so that the one closest to the CPU is serviced first

daisy–wheel printer an IMPACT PRINTER that prints FULLY FORMED CHARACTERS one at a time by rotating a circular print element composed of a series of individual spokes, each containing two characters, that radiate out from a center hub: daisy–wheel printers are widely used with WORD PROCESSORS

DASD (DAZ dee) acronym for DIRECT ACCESS STORAGE DEVICE

data characters grouped together in specific patterns, to which meaning is assigned: commonly used to designate the numbers, facts, concepts, or the like to be processed by a program although any information input to a computer system is considered data

data access arrangement an electrical interface device required by telephone companies when customer–owned terminals and their related equipment are connected to the direct–dial telephone network   Compare CONNECTING ARRANGEMENT

data administrator a person who controls the selection of data stored in various files and coordinates its use

data aggregate a named group of fields within a record, such as a date containing the month, day, and year, or a repeating group, such as a number of withdrawals and deposits

data attribute ATTRIBUTE

data bank **1** all the data files readily available for use in a specific computer center: for example, a company's payroll, personnel records, accounts payable/receivable, and inventory files could be considered a data bank **2** one data file compiled from a variety of sources on one subject: for example, if birth records, school records, employment records, and tax records were collected for a group of individuals and stored in one data file, it would be considered a data bank **3** loosely, DATA BASE

data base **1** a set of interrelated data records stored on a DIRECT ACCESS STORAGE DEVICE in a data structure that is designed to allow multiple applications to access the data, to have minimal redundancy of data, and to allow for growth and change: a data base is a highly structured file that attempts to provide all the data allocated to a subject and to allow programs to use only those items they need: for example, a data base in a university that contains faculty information can be used by different programs to print payroll checks, assign teachers to classrooms, and so on **2** loosely, a FILE or DATA BANK

data base administrator a professional who determines the way in which data is organized in the data base, assigns names and definitions to the various records and fields, oversees the security system of the data base, and is responsible for controlling all information placed in or deleted from the data base

data base management system a collection of software that handles the storage, retrieval, and updating of records in a data base: a data base management system controls redundancy of records and provides the security, integrity, and data independence of a data base

data bus a bus that transfers words from one location in the computer to another, as from the CPU to main memory See SYSTEM BUS

data carrier DATA MEDIUM

data cell 1 a magazine containing strips of magnetized tape for the storage of data: a group of data cells make up a DIRECT ACCESS STORAGE DEVICE called a **data cell drive**. Data cell drives offer tremendous storage capacity at a relatively low cost, but each strip must be mechanically withdrawn from the magazine and wrapped around a drum in order to read or write data, making the ACCESS TIME much slower than, for example, that of disk storage **2** MEMORY CELL

data channel INPUT/OUTPUT CHANNEL

data check an error in the data read caused by a flaw on the recording surface of a medium such as magnetic tape or disk: the error cannot be corrected at that place, and that portion of the recording surface cannot be used again

data collection the gathering and recording of data for processing by a computer

data collection system a teleprocessing system in which items of data are entered on various terminals and stored in a central computer for immediate or subsequent processing: an example of a data collection system is a bank using many terminals to enter transactions as they occur. These transactions are either stored for overnight processing or are immediately entered against the individual accounts Compare DATA DISTRIBUTION SYSTEM

Datacom a data communication service offered by Western Union for relatively low–cost transmission, currently connecting approximately sixty cities in the United States

data communications the transmission and reception of coded data in a computer system according to the rules of a specific PROTOCOL

data communications equipment the equipment providing the necessary functions, such as establishing and terminating a connection between two devices and performing the necessary code conversions in transmitting data

data communications processor an INPUT/ OUTPUT CHANNEL that sends data to and receives data from a number of remote terminals connected to the computer system through telephone lines or other communications lines, such as COAXIAL CABLE

data communication terminal TERMINAL

data compaction DATA COMPRESSION

data compression the elimination of blanks, unnecessary fields, and redundant data from various records in order to reduce the amount of storage needed

data control the function performed by personnel in a computer center in controlling the execution of various jobs by preparing machine–readable data from source documents, scheduling the execution of jobs, and distributing the output to users

data control block a block containing information about the name and description of a file stored in a computer system, as well as an address that points to additional information about the file

data conversion 1 the process of converting data from one machine–readable form to another, as from card to tape or tape to disk **2** the process of changing data in one code to another code, as from ASCII to EBCDIC, when transferring data from one type of equipment to another

data definition statement a JCL statement giving information about a file, such as its name and whether it is stored on disk or tape Compare EXECUTE STATEMENT, JOB STATEMENT

data descriptor 1 in an assembly language program, a programming statement used to define constants or reserve storage locations in main memory **2** KEYWORD

data distribution system a teleprocessing system in which items of data stored in a central computer system are sent to various terminals continuously, in groups, or on demand: an example of a data distribution system is one in which stock market quotations and transactions are distributed to various terminals in stock brokerages Compare DATA COLLECTION SYSTEM

data element FIELD

data entry 1 the process of entering data into a device that converts it to a form that can be read by the computer, as by typing on a keypunch, terminal, or a KEY-TO-DISK or KEY-TO-TAPE system **2** the process of putting data into a computer for processing

data entry mode INPUT MODE

data field FIELD

data file FILE

data-formatting statements programming statements that define the FORMAT of data to be processed in a program

data hierarchy the structure of data into sets and subsets in an ordered sequence: for example, a bit is part of a byte, a byte is part of a word, and so on

data item 1 FIELD **2** the value found in a field

data link the equipment, such as a DATA SINK and DATA SOURCE, and the protocol that allow information in data format to be transmitted from one location to another

data link control the communications control characters that initiate a connection between two locations, check for errors, and terminate the transmission of the data

data link escape an ESCAPE CHARACTER preceding communications control characters during the transmission of data in order to distinguish them from other data

data management programs INPUT/OUTPUT CONTROL SYSTEM

data management system a group of programs that provide for the creation and maintenance of files, for the production of reports from them, and for handling a wide variety of different types of data structures

data manipulation the sorting, merging, editing, and other such processing of data in order to facilitate further use of it

data medium any of the various storage devices used in a computer system, such as paper tape, magnetic tape, punched cards, or disk

data organization DATA STRUCTURE

data origination SOURCE DATA AUTOMATION

Dataphone a trademark for any of various data communications devices and services offered by AT & T

data plotter PLOTTER

data preparation the process of converting data into machine-readable form, as in keypunching it onto cards, so that it can be input to the computer

data processing the use of a computer and its peripheral devices, such as disk drives, terminals, and printers, to process data automatically by sorting, classifying, summarizing, and performing other such procedures at high rates of speed: the general term in use for business applications of the computer

data processing center COMPUTER CENTER

data protection FILE PROTECTION

data record RECORD (sense 1)

data reduction the process of condensing RAW DATA into an ordered or simplified form that can then be more easily entered onto a storage medium and processed by a program

data register MEMORY DATA REGISTER

data representation the machine-readable form in which data has been recorded, such as Hollerith code on punch cards

data security SECURITY

data set **1** a named collection of logically related records stored in a data structure, that is efficient for processing and is described by control information, such as the record length, the block size, the data set label, and the record format: a data set is considered to be the major unit of storage in a computer system. Although the terms **file** and **data set** are sometimes used interchangeably, **file** generally refers to any collection of data, whereas **data set** is applied more specifically to a collection of records that have already been stored **2** MODEM

data set control block a block containing the name, description, and location of a data set stored on a disk

data set label (abbreviated DSL) a label that describes such attributes of a data set as its name, size, read/write privileges, and physical boundaries in storage: the label is entered at the beginning of a tape for data sets stored on tape and in a VTOC for data sets on disk

data set name a name, specified by the programmer, according to conventions established by a computer center, that identifies a specific data set and is used in subsequent programs that access the data set

data set ready a pin on an interface for a modem indicating whether the modem is connected to a communication channel and is ready to exchange control characters to initiate data transmission: one of the standards used by RS–232–C and CCITT V.24

data sheet SOURCE DOCUMENT

data signal rate selector a pin on an interface for a modem used to select either of two rates at which signals are to be sent or received in synchronous transmission or any of a range of rates for asynchronous transmission, usually expressed in bits per second: one of the standards used by RS–232–C. In CCITT V.24, the corresponding pin is called **data signaling rate selector**

data sink　the device receiving and responding to data transmitted by a data source

data source　the device responsible for originating the transmission of data

data stream　the data transferred in a single read or write operation

data structure　any of various forms of organization of records in a file, such as a LIST or TREE

data tablet　in COMPUTER GRAPHICS, a tablet used to input data by moving a hand–held stylus over its surface and drawing images that are transmitted in the form of lines or dots to the computer for storage and for displaying on a CRT, where its shape can be manipulated

data terminal equipment　the equipment needed to support the transmission of data from a terminal, such as the DATA SINK and DATA SOURCE

data terminal ready　a pin on an interface for a modem that prepares and maintains the connection to a communication channel: one of the standards used by RS–232–C and CCITT V.24

data transfer rate　TRANSFER RATE

data transmission　the sending of data from one location in a computer system to another in the form of electrical signals that define a bit by the strength and duration of the signal

data transmission system　the various pieces of hardware and software used to transmit data from one location to another

data type the classification of an item of data, as to whether it is composed of integers, letters, or real numbers

data verification the process of determining whether data has been accurately collected and recorded, performed by visual and other checks, such as record counts, hash totals, and limit checks

data word a WORD containing data to be processed by an instruction Compare INSTRUCTION WORD

datum a unit of data

DBMS abbreviation for DATA BASE MANAGEMENT SYSTEM

DCB abbreviation for DATA CONTROL BLOCK

DCE abbreviation for DATA COMMUNICATIONS EQUIPMENT

DDD abbreviation for DIRECT DISTANCE DIALING

dd name a label identifying a specific DATA DEFINITION STATEMENT

DDP abbreviation for DISTRIBUTED DATA PROCESSING

dd statement DATA DEFINITION STATEMENT

deadlock a condition occurring in a multiprogramming system when two or more programs in main memory cannot continue to execute because each is waiting for a resource held by another: for example, if program A is waiting for a tape drive assigned to program B and program B is waiting for a disk assigned to program A, and neither can complete execution until the other releases its resource, then a deadlock has occurred. Multiprogramming systems normally have methods to prevent or to detect and resolve deadlocks

deadly embrace DEADLOCK

deallocate   to release a resource previously assigned to a program so that it is available for use by another program

deblocking   the process of isolating the logical records from one another in a block   Compare BLOCKING

debug   to trace and correct errors in programming code or hardware malfunctions in a computer system

debug aids   a prewritten set of computerized routines that provides information to help a programmer or computer engineer in the tracing of bugs

decentralized data processing   DATA PROCESSING in an organization where the processing and storage of data are provided independently at various locations throughout the organization   See DISTRIBUTED DATA PROCESSING   Compare CENTRALIZED DATA PROCESSING

decimal   designating a situation in which there is a choice of ten different possible values or states

decimal digit   any one of the 10 digits in the decimal number system, represented by 0, 1, 2, 3, 4, 5, 6, 7, 8, or 9

decimal number   a number in the decimal number system represented by one or more decimal digits

decimal number system   the base 10 number system that represents a decimal number as the sum of successive powers of 10: for example, the decimal number 4239 can be expressed as $(4 \times 10^3) + (2 \times 10^2) + (3 \times 10^1) + (9 \times 10^0)$, where $10^0 = 1$

decimal point   the RADIX POINT in a decimal number that has an integer (or an implied integer value of 0, as in .25) and a fractional part: for example, 10.25

decipher to reconstruct the original data from previously enciphered data Compare ENCIPHER

decision the computer process of taking any of alternative courses of action based on specific conditions: for example, in calculating a payroll, decisions are made based on whether each employee is salaried or paid by the hour

decision table a table of the operations a computer will be used to perform and the conditions under which those operations should be performed in order to solve a particular problem: a decision table can be used as an alternative to a flowchart in representing the various steps taken in a program

declarative statement NONEXECUTABLE STATEMENT

decode to interpret a code: for example, the number 0110 is coded in BCD and can be decoded to the decimal number 6 Compare ENCODE

decoder a circuit used to interpret a specific code: for example, a control unit has a decoder to interpret the OP CODE of a machine instruction in order to determine the operations needed to execute the instruction Compare ENCODER

decollator see CONTINUOUS FORMS

decrement 1 a quantity subtracted from another quantity 2 to subtract a quantity, usually 1, from another quantity: for example, in keeping track of loop executions, the counter can be set at the final figure and decremented by 1 with each execution Compare INCREMENT

decrypt DECIPHER

dedicated designating a resource that is reserved for a particular program, function, or user

default a value, parameter, attribute, or option that is assigned by the program or system when another has not been specified by the user

define to assign meaning to a constant or variable in a program by describing its length and data type

degauss to erase the data recorded on a magnetic tape: data is normally replaced with new data rather than erased

delay line a circuit that temporarily stores a bit by delaying its transmission for a specified interval of time

delete key a key that eliminates a character from the screen of a CRT and moves all the following characters in the line one position to the left

deletion record in updating a master file, a record that removes an existing record from the file

delimiter **1** a special character that designates the end of a field, record, or string **2** a special character, often a #, used to separate items of data, that is, strings of characters

demand paging a technique by which a page is brought into main memory only when it is needed by the program See PAGE FAULT

demodulation the process of converting analog data to digital data, as by receiving tones sent over a communication line and reconverting them to the original bits See MODEM

demultiplexer a device that connects a single input line to any of several output lines Compare MULTIPLEXER

dense binary code a binary code in which all possible bit patterns are used to represent characters, as opposed to one in which certain patterns have no meaning

dense list a list in which all possible cells are filled: a record cannot be added to a dense list until more storage space has been allocated to the list or another record is deleted

density the number of bits or characters that can be recorded in a given length of recording surface: expressed in bits or bytes per inch

deque (DECK) a list that allows insertions and deletions at both ends: a deque is considered to be **input–restricted** when insertions may be made at only one end but deletions may be made at either end, and **output–restricted** when deletions may be made at only one end but insertions may be made at either end Compare QUEUE, STACK

dequeue to remove items from a QUEUE

descending sort a sorting technique that arranges items in a highest to lowest sequence

descriptor KEYWORD

desk checking the process of manually working through a program with a small set of sample data before executing it on the computer, in order to detect any errors in its logic or syntax

desktop computer MICROCOMPUTER

destination the device to which data is being sent

destructive read a READ that destroys the contents of a storage location by changing the bits to all zeros or all ones: also called a **destructive readout** Compare NONDESTRUCTIVE READ

detail file TRANSACTION FILE

device a combination of physical components forming a unit that performs a specific function, such as storage or input/output

device independence designating the ability to write programs without taking into account the specific characteristics of the input/output device being used

device number a number assigned to a particular peripheral device, that is used to identify it in the computer

diagnostic 1 an ERROR MESSAGE printed in a program listing by a compiler or an assembler **2** designating the detection and isolation of an error in a program or a malfunction in equipment

diagnostic routine a routine designed to locate a malfunction in computer equipment or an error in a program

diagnostic test the execution of a diagnostic routine that checks all or selected parts of a device, such as a printer, in order to detect failures by comparing the results with known correct results

dial–up line a communication line that connects a terminal and the computer when a person dials a specified phone number to make the connection: the data is transmitted over various telephone lines to the computer, and the person is usually charged for the length of time the connection is made Compare LEASED LINE

dial–up terminal a terminal that is connected to a computer through a dial–up line and can therefore be used in any location where a suitable telephone connection can be made

dibit a pair of bits: 00, 01, 10, or 11

dichotomizing search a search in which a file is divided into two equal or unequal parts, one of which is determined to contain the desired record and the other discarded: the retained portion is then split again, and the process is continued until the desired record is found See BINARY SEARCH, FIBONACCI SEARCH

dictionary 1 TABLE **2** a list of the labels or keys used in a program and a description of their logical meanings for documentation purposes

digit any of the symbols representing the positive integers in some numbering system, such as 0 to 9 in the decimal number system or 0 and 1 in the binary number system See BIT, DECIMAL DIGIT, HEXADECIMAL DIGIT

digital referring to the binary representation of numerical quantities by the number of discrete physical signals, or by the presence or absence of those signals in particular positions Compare ANALOG

digital computer a computer that performs its tasks by noting the presence or absence of physical signals in a particular position: this on or off condition represents binary data that can be manipulated arithmetically or logically to produce a solution. Digital computers are used primarily for administrative data processing and mathematical computation and are the most commonly used computers

digital data discrete data, such as integers or other discontinuous characters, represented by specific patterns of binary digits Compare ANALOG DATA

digital recording a technique of recording in which sounds are converted into digital bits representing the amplitude of the signal at each of about 40,000 equal intervals per second and recorded on a small thin disk or on tape: the bits are read by a narrow, low-power laser beam and reproduced as the original sounds

digital-to-analog converter a device that converts data in digital form to the corresponding analog signals Compare ANALOG–TO–DIGITAL CON-VERTER

digitize 1 to translate analog data into digital data **2** to assign a digital number to a character or symbol

digit punch a punched hole in any of the rows zero through nine of an 80–COLUMN CARD: for example, a punch in the seven–row represents the digit 7 See HOLLERITH CODE Compare ZONE PUNCH

dimension the defined size of an array: for example, the dimension of an array with three rows and four columns is (3,4) or 3 by 4

DIP acronym for DUAL–IN–LINE PACKAGE

direct access designating a storage medium that allows items of data to be directly accessed without having to access items that precede them in storage Compare SEQUENTIAL ACCESS

direct access method a RANDOM ACCESS METHOD in which records are accessed by their known address: in a direct access method only one SEEK and one READ–WRITE are required to access a record Compare SEQUENTIAL ACCESS METHOD

direct access storage device a storage device, such as a magnetic disk or drum, that provides direct access to the data stored on it and has an ACCESS TIME that is not dependent on the location of the data Compare SEQUENTIAL STORAGE DEVICE

direct addressing an addressing mode in which the address of a storage location containing data for an instruction is specified in the instruction

direct distance dialing a service offered by telephone companies allowing direct dialing for data communications between most points in the public telephone system

direct file a file whose records are stored in a random order on a DIRECT ACCESS STORAGE DEVICE, thereby allowing them to be retrieved in any order

direct memory access a method for transferring data directly to and from main memory, bypassing the CPU: such a method does not require software to keep track of memory addresses and, therefore, greatly improves the transfer rate

direct memory access channel an input/output channel used for the transfer of data between main memory and high–speed peripheral devices

directory INDEX

direct read after write DRAW

disable to set various switches or enter various commands in order to prevent a processor from accepting certain types of interrupts, such as those that indicate data is ready to be sent or received Compare ENABLE

discrete data data in the form of whole numbers that represent distinct values, as the numbers of employees in various departments Compare CONTINUOUS DATA

discrete programming INTEGER PROGRAMMING

disjunction an OR operation

disk, disc clipped form of MAGNETIC DISK a platter, resembling a phonograph record, coated with a material capable of being magnetized to store bits in concentric circular paths, called TRACKS, on either of its surfaces: each disk commonly has two hundred or more tracks and is arranged with a number of other disks into a stack. When so grouped, the disks are called a DISK PACK. A disk is the most common type of DIRECT ACCESS STORAGE DEVICE

disk drive a unit that reads and writes data stored on a disk: the drive rapidly rotates all the disks in a disk pack and has a number of ACCESS ARMS that are placed between each pair of adjacent disks. Generally both sides of each disk are used for data except for the top surface of the first disk and the bottom surface of the last in the pack

diskette FLOPPY DISK

disk operating system an operating system stored on disk, rather than in main memory, when the computer is operating

disk pack a storage unit containing a number of disks supported by a center spindle with about a half inch between disks: the disk pack can be made up of FIXED DISKS or REMOVABLE DISKS

disk sector a pie shaped area on the surface of some disks: the sectors divide each track into a number of sections, each of which can store a specified number of characters, commonly 512. Each BLOCK must begin on the boundary of a sector, and a block length as close to 512 as possible is desirable in order to use all available storage space on a track. Each sector is numbered and used as the address for directly accessing a block

dispatcher a program in the OPERATING SYSTEM that chooses the next task to execute from the group of currently active tasks after an interrupt has occurred

dispatching the scheduling of the CPU for use by the various active programs

displacement the arithmetic difference between the address of a storage location in main memory and another known address

display 1 a visual representation of data, as on the screen of a CRT 2 to so present data

display unit VIDEO DISPLAY UNIT

distributed data processing DATA PROCESSING in an organization where some or all of the processing and storage of data is provided at different locations that are connected by telecommunication lines See DECENTRALIZED DATA PROCESSING

distributed network a network in which communication between various terminals and computers may take place through alternative communication lines Compare STAR NETWORK, RING NETWORK, TREE NETWORK

divide exception an EXCEPTION created when the signed number resulting from a division would cause overflow

DLC abbreviation for DATA LINK CONTROL

DMA abbreviation for DIRECT MEMORY ACCESS

DMAC (DEE mack) acronym for DIRECT MEMORY ACCESS CHANNEL

DO a programming word in high–level languages that precedes a statement (or statements) to be executed when a specified condition is met

document 1 SOURCE DOCUMENT 2 to prepare DOCUMENTATION

documentation a collection of written descriptions and procedures that provide information and guidance about a program or about all or part of a computer system so that it can be properly used and maintained

DOS (DOSS) acronym for DISK OPERATING SYSTEM

dot–matrix character a printed character formed of dots so close together that it gives the impression of having been printed by uninterrupted strokes: the dots are formed by wire ends, jets of ink, electrical charge, or laser beams Compare FULLY FORMED CHARACTERS

dot–matrix printer WIRE–MATRIX PRINTER

double buffering a technique in which two buffers are used to hold data being transferred from one device to another: when buffer A is being emptied, buffer B is being filled, and so on until the transfer is complete

double–dabble a method for converting binary numbers to their decimal equivalents by doubling the bit to the far left, adding the next bit, doubling the sum, and so on until the sum contains the rightmost bit: for example, the binary number 101 is converted as follows: $1 \times 2 = 2$, $2 + 0 = 2$, $2 \times 2 = 4$, $4 + 1 = 5$

double–density recording a technique in which the density of bits recorded on a magnetic storage medium, such as tape or disk, can be doubled by modifying the amplitude and frequency of the write signal

double–length designating an item of data made up of two words

double–precision designating the use of two words to store an item of data when they are needed to maintain a higher level of precision Compare SINGLE–PRECISION, TRIPLE–PRECISION

double punch two digit punches in a column of a punch card: often used as a control punch

double–sided floppy a floppy disk that can have data recorded on either side: the floppy is either removed from the drive and flipped over to access data on the other side or it is inserted into a special drive for accessing data on either surface

double word two adjacent WORDS used to store data that is more than can be represented in one word Compare HALF WORD, FULL WORD

DO–WHILE a programming statement in a high–level language that is used to perform the instructions in a loop while a certain condition exists, as while variable X is less than 10

down designating a computer, a component of a computer system, or a software system that is not operating correctly due to an error or malfunction and so is not available for use Compare UP

downtime the period during which a computer, a component of a computer system, or a software system is down Compare UPTIME

downward compatible designating an older version of a computer or software system, such as a language processor, that produces identical results for a program executed on a newer version Compare UPWARD COMPATIBLE

DP abbreviation for DATA PROCESSING

DRAW acronym for **D**IRECT **R**EAD **A**FTER **W**RITE an operation in which data recorded on a video disk is read immediately after it is recorded so that errors can be detected: errors cannot be erased or written over on this type of disk, but the data can be corrected and rewritten at a new location. The computer is then directed to the new location so that the section containing the error is ignored

drive a unit that reads and writes data on an external storage device, such as a DISK DRIVE or a MAGNETIC TAPE DRIVE

driver 1 a program that controls devices or other programs 2 an electrical element that increases the power or current that a circuit can handle

drop the telephone line connecting a user's remote terminal to a communication line, such as a telephone cable

drop in an error in which extra bits are read or recorded on a magnetic storage device, such as tape Compare DROP OUT

drop out an error in which one or more bits fail to be read or recorded on a magnetic storage device, such as tape Compare DROP IN

drum MAGNETIC DRUM

drum plotter a PLOTTER consisting of paper wrapped around a horizontal drum that can rotate either forward or backward, and a pen suspended over the paper that can move from side to side: the combined movements of the drum and pen produce short lines that can be connected to form straight lines, curved lines, or characters

drum printer an IMPACT PRINTER that prints a line of FULLY FORMED CHARACTERS by striking an inked ribbon and paper against a rapidly rotating drum: the drum contains a complete set of embossed characters that circle it at each print position, forming a row of A's, B's, etc., across its surface. As the drum rotates, all the A's in the line are printed, all the B's, etc., until it has made a complete revolution

DSCB abbreviation for DATA SET CONTROL BLOCK

DSN abbreviation for DATA SET NAME

DTE abbreviation for DATA TERMINAL EQUIPMENT

DTR abbreviation for DATA TERMINAL READY

dual–in–line package the most common type of integrated circuit on a chip, having two parallel rows of seven pins each

dual processors MASTER–SLAVE SYSTEM

dumb terminal a terminal that provides only for the input and output of data to and from the computer and cannot be programmed to perform other functions   Compare INTELLIGENT TERMINAL

dummy an artificial instruction, address, etc. used only to fulfill specifications in a program but not actually performing a function

dump   **1** a copy of the contents of storage locations in main memory at a specified point in time, that is recorded on paper, tape, or disk: the contents of memory are most commonly represented in hexadecimal notation, and it is used for debugging purposes   **2** to record on paper, tape, or disk the contents of main memory at a specified point in time   **3** to transfer the entire contents of a file from one type of storage medium onto another, as from disk to tape

duodecimal designating a situation in which there is a choice of twelve different possible values or states

duplex FULL–DUPLEX

duplex channel a communication channel that allows data to be transmitted in both directions simultaneously

duplexing the practice of keeping duplicate devices as standby units in case of a failure in a primary unit

duplication REPRODUCTION

dyadic operation an operation involving two operands: for example, A+B is a dyadic operation involving the two operands, A and B, which are separated by the dyadic operator for addition, +

dyadic operator an arithmetic or logical operator that connects two operands: the valid dyadic operators are the arithmetic operators +, –, *, / and the logical operators AND, OR, NAND, NOT, XOR, and NOR

dynamic designating an event that occurs during the execution of a program

dynamic address translator a hardware device that converts a VIRTUAL ADDRESS into a REAL ADDRESS

dynamic allocation the allocation of resources as they are needed during the execution of a program Compare STATIC ALLOCATION

dynamic dump a dump performed during the execution of a program, usually at points specified by the programmer for debugging purposes

dynamic programming in OPERATIONS RESEARCH, a technique for finding the optimal solution to a problem by having a number of decisions available at each step of the program: every decision is made on the basis of its effect on the overall problem and helps to determine the decision at the next step

dynamic RAM a RAM that must be periodically refreshed since the stored data tends to fade with time Compare STATIC RAM

dynamic relocation in a multiprogramming system, the movement of a program to different sets of storage locations each time it is brought into main memory for further execution Compare STATIC RELOCATION

dynamic storage DYNAMIC RAM

dynamic storage allocation the allocation of storage locations in main memory to a program as needed during its execution, which are released when no longer needed by the program Compare STATIC STORAGE ALLOCATION

dynamic subroutine a subroutine in SKELETAL CODE that is completed with various adjustments by the computer during the course of the program, such as the positioning of a decimal point

E

E in the HEXADECIMAL NUMBER SYSTEM, the symbol that corresponds to the decimal number 14

EAROM (EAR rom) acronym for **E**LECTRICALLY **A**LTERABLE **R**EAD–**O**NLY **M**EMORY a type of ROM that can be erased and reprogrammed without having to be removed from the circuit board: an EAROM is reprogrammed electrically and, although more expensive, is a more convenient, faster method than the one used to reprogram an EPROM Compare PROM, EPROM

EBCDIC (EBB suh dik) acronym for **E**XTENDED **BI**NARY **C**ODED **D**ECIMAL **I**NTERCHANGE **C**ODE a standard eight–bit code (with a ninth bit used as a parity bit) for the representation of characters: the eight bits permit the representation of 256 characters, including upper and lower case letters of the alphabet, numbers, and special symbols. EBCDIC is the standard code used on IBM equipment

echo 1 a copy of a record printed in the program listing by the compiler as the record is read **2** part of a transmitted signal that returns to the sending location and causes interference in data that is subsequently transmitted

echo check 1 a visual check performed by a programmer on the echoes in a program listing to ensure accuracy **2** a test performed by transmitting data just received back to the sending location for comparison with the original data in order to check the accuracy

edit to make changes, additions, or deletions in a file containing a program and/or data

edit mode a mode of operation for a terminal in which files consisting of programs and/or data may be modified Compare INPUT MODE, COMMAND MODE

editor a program that provides the capability of editing a program and/or data stored as a file without rewriting the entire file: a terminal is commonly used to access an editor so that the file can be viewed while the editing is performed

EDP abbreviation for ELECTRONIC DATA PROCESSING

EEROM (EE rom) acronym for **E**LECTRICALLY **E**RASABLE **R**EAD–**O**NLY **M**EMORY another term for EAROM

effective address the absolute address that is derived by modifying the ADDRESS PART of an instruction through an addressing mode, such as RELATIVE ADDRESSING or INDIRECT ADDRESSING, and is used as the actual address of the operand

EIA abbreviation for ELECTRONIC INDUSTRIES ASSOCIATION an organization of electronics manufacturers that sets standards for the electrical and functional characteristics of equipment used in data communications See RS–232–C

80–column card a PUNCH CARD that is 7 3/8 inches long and 3 1/4 inches wide and contains 80 columns and 12 rows: the columns are numbered 1 through 80 from left to right; the rows are named, from top to bottom, twelve–row, eleven–row, and the zero through nine rows. A character is represented by a unique combination of punched holes in a column See HOL-

LERITH CODE, ELEVEN–PUNCH, TWELVE–PUNCH, ZERO PUNCH, ZONE PUNCH, DIGIT PUNCH

elastic buffer a buffer that can hold a variable amount of data depending upon the need at any given time

electrically erasable read–only memory EAROM

electronic data processing AUTOMATIC DATA PROCESSING in which an electronic machine, such as a digital computer, operating at electronic speeds, is used to perform a series of operations on data

electronic mail letters, memos, or text typed into a terminal and transmitted to a receiving terminal or terminals, where it can be displayed at the viewer's choice of time or at some prearranged time

electrosensitive printer ELECTROSTATIC PRINTER

electrostatic printer a NONIMPACT PRINTER that prints DOT-MATRIX CHARACTERS one at a time by means of wires or pins that supply an electrical charge in the desired patterns onto an aluminum–coated paper: particles of dry ink adhere to the magnetized areas and are then fixed by heat

electrostatic storage a storage medium, as for the screen of a CRT, that stores bits in the form of charged areas

electrothermal printer THERMAL PRINTER

elegant designating a program efficiently written to use the smallest possible amount of main memory by decreasing the number of instructions used to accomplish various tasks

element **1** any of the units comprising a larger item **2** one item of data in an array

elementary gate GATE

elementary item a term most commonly used to describe a field in COBOL

eleven–punch a punched hole in the second row, called the eleven–row, of an 80–COLUMN CARD See ZONE PUNCH

emulator a set of microprograms that can be used in a computer to perform the functions of, or execute programs designed for, another, different type of computer: a computer with an emulator can run programs in its own machine language or in the machine language of another computer

enable to set various switches or enter various commands in order to allow a processor to accept certain types of interrupts, such as those that indicate data is ready to be sent or received Compare DISABLE

encipher **1** to scramble information according to predefined rules so that it cannot be read without knowledge of them, as in the transmission of data over communication lines **2** the process of so scrambling information

encode to convert data into a code: for example, the decimal number 2 can be encoded to the BCD number 0010 Compare DECODE

encoder a circuit that encodes: for example, a terminal has an encoder to convert a signal, received when a key is depressed on the keyboard, into the corresponding code, such as ASCII or EBCDIC, for that key

encrypt ENCIPHER

END a programming statement signaling the end of statements to be executed, as at the end of a program, a loop, or the statements following a DO .

end–around carry a carry resulting from the addition of two HIGH–ORDER BITS that is added into the LOW–ORDER BIT

end–around shift CIRCULAR SHIFT

endless loop INFINITE LOOP

end of file EOF

end of message EOM

end–of–tape marker a marker used to indicate the end of the available recording area on a magnetic tape: it is generally a reflective strip, about an inch in length, that is sensed photoelectrically when it passes over a light beam on a tape drive

end of text a communications control character indicating the end of data being transmitted in a message

end of transmission a communications control character indicating the end of transmission

end of transmission block a communications control character used to signal the end of transmission of a block of data

end user the ultimate user of the output produced by a program or system

ENQ abbreviation for ENQUIRY CHARACTER

enqueue to enter items into a QUEUE

enquiry character a communications control character used to request the identification and/or status of a sending or receiving device

enter key a key on some terminals that is used to transfer the line or lines of data that have just been typed to the computer for processing and to return the cursor (or print mechanism on a terminal that has paper instead of a CRT) to the first position on the next line: also called a **return key** on some terminals

entry point the address of the first instruction in a program, routine, or subroutine, where execution begins Compare REENTRY POINT

environment the operating conditions under which a computer system is designed to operate, such as a multiprogramming or multiprocessing environment

EOF abbreviation for END OF FILE a control character indicating that the last record in a file has been read

EOM abbreviation for END OF MESSAGE a communications control character signaling the end of a message

EOT abbreviation for **1** END OF TRANSMISSION **2** END-OF-TAPE MARKER

EPROM (EE prom) acronym for **E**RASABLE **P**ROGRAMMABLE **R**EAD-**O**NLY **M**EMORY a type of ROM that can be erased and reprogrammed by the customer: an EPROM can have its bit patterns erased by exposing it to a high-intensity, ultraviolet light for a period of time, usually 15 to 20 minutes. Once this has been done, all the bits are erased and the EPROM may be reprogrammed. This makes an EPROM particularly useful during the program development stage of a system Compare PROM, EAROM

EQ an abbreviation for EQUAL TO, used as a relational operator in a program

equalization CONDITIONING

equation an arithmetic statement consisting of two expressions, connected by an equal sign (=), that have equality, as in $a+b = b+a$

equivalence gate EXCLUSIVE-NOR GATE

equivalent binary digits the number of bits needed to represent a number in a different base while maintaining the same precision: an average of 3 1/2 times more bits are needed to represent a decimal number in binary form

erasable storage a storage medium, such as a disk or magnetic tape, that can be reused to store different data

error in a computer system, any deviation of a quantity from the known, correct value, such as a truncation error or a parity error, whether of human or machine origin Compare MALFUNC-TION, MISTAKE

error condition a condition resulting from an error, such as an attempt to execute an illegal instruction or to divide by zero

error control in data communications, a process that detects errors in the transmission of MES-SAGES, requests the retransmission of faulty messages, and accepts correct messages: error control is handled by the particular PROTOCOL of the communication system

error control character ACCURACY CONTROL CHARACTER

error–correcting code a code that, by including extra parity bits in the data for use in repeated parity checks, can detect and correct certain types of errors that may occur when data is read, written, or transmitted: the pattern of parity check failures points directly to the bit that is in error, and the bit is changed to its opposite value, that is, from a 1 to 0 or vice versa

error–detecting code a code with additional bits, such as parity bits, so that when the data is read, written, or transmitted, errors can be detected and the data can be retransmitted

error file a file created during the execution of a program to store those records containing errors as detected by the program: this file is then usually printed so that the records can be visually scanned for the errors

error message a printed description of an error found in a program during its translation into machine language by an assembler or compiler or found in the data during execution of the program

error rate a measure of the quality of a circuit or transmission system: it is determined by dividing the number of erroneous items of data received by the total number of items received

error recovery procedures procedures that assist in isolating and, where possible, correcting malfunctions in equipment

error report 1 a printout of records containing data on malfunctions that have occurred in a computer system: the data is recorded on disk as the malfunctions occur, and the report is then periodically produced for use by the personnel responsible for the maintenance of equipment 2 a printout of those records in a file found, during the execution of the program, to contain an error

ESC abbreviation for ESCAPE CHARACTER

escape character a character that causes the characters that follow it to be interpreted differently from those preceding it: for example, an escape character can be used to indicate that subsequent characters are to be interpreted by a different code or that they are not to be treated as data but as control characters

ETB abbreviation for END OF TRANSMISSION BLOCK

ETX abbreviation for END OF TEXT

even parity see PARITY BIT

event 1 TRANSACTION 2 an occurrence during the execution of a task, such as the completion of an input/output operation

exception a condition caused by an attempt to execute an invalid operation, such as dividing by zero, that normally causes an interrupt

excess–n notation a notation in which a binary number, x, is represented as x + n: for example, excess–64 notation is used in IBM computers for representing the exponent of floating–point numbers so that they have a positive value. The negative exponent –2 can be represented as –2 + 64 or 62 and eliminates the need for a sign bit in the exponent portion of the number. The value of 64 is chosen since the number of bits used to represent the exponent can hold a binary number in the range of 0 to +127 and the exponent can then have a value in the range of –64 to +63

exclusive–NOR gate a GATE that produces an output signal of 1 when both input signals are 1 or both input signals are 0; otherwise the output signal is 0

exclusive–OR XOR

exclusive–OR gate XOR GATE

executable form a program that has been either written in, or translated by a language processor into, machine language and that is ready for execution by the computer

executable statement a programming statement in a high–level language that specifies an operation to be performed on data   Compare NONEXECUTABLE STATEMENT

execute to perform the operations indicated in an instruction on the specified data

execute statement the job control language statement that executes a program (or programs) by identifying the appropriate load module or procedure: for example, an execute statement is used to identify the COMPILER that will be used by the program

execution   the process of carrying out the operations specified in the instructions of a program

execution cycle   the sequence of events by which the operation specified by an instruction is performed on the operands See INSTRUCTION CYCLE

execution time   **1** the amount of time required to perform an execution cycle **2** the phase during which a program is being executed **3** the time required to fetch, decode, and execute an instruction

executive program SUPERVISOR

exit point   the address of the instruction in a program that transfers control to a subroutine

expandable   designating a computer that is capable of having its storage capacity increased with the addition of more main memory and/or disk drives

explicit address ABSOLUTE ADDRESS

expression   in a program, a combination of various constants, variables, operators, and parentheses used to perform a desired computation

extended punched–card code HOLLERITH CODE

extensible language   a programming language that allows users to add new features or to modify existing ones in order to tailor the language to their requirements

extent   an amount of contiguous space on a DIRECT ACCESS STORAGE DEVICE reserved for a file

external memory AUXILIARY STORAGE

external reference   the name of a variable, constant, or program module used in a module other than the one in which its length and data type were specified: a LINKAGE EDITOR is used to resolve external references

external sort a sort in which an external storage device is used to store intermediate groups of sorted items when the entire group is too large to be sorted in main memory: the intermediate groups are then merged in several steps to form the final sorted group once each has been internally sorted Compare INTERNAL SORT

external storage AUXILIARY STORAGE

external symbol dictionary a symbol table containing the symbolic names of the various modules of a program and their addresses

extraction the process of selecting various components from a storage unit, as records from a file, fields from a record, or bits from a word, in order to form a new unit that can be separately analyzed or processed

F

F in the HEXADECIMAL NUMBER SYSTEM, the symbol that corresponds to the decimal number 15

facsimile FAX

fail–safe designating a system that continues to operate after a malfunction occurs, usually with a reduction in speed

fail–soft designating a computer system that will continue operating at a reduced level when a part of the system fails, but that will provide substantial warning so that irrecoverable loss of data does not occur

false code **1** ILLEGAL CHARACTER **2** an instruction specifying an ILLEGAL OPERATION

fanfold paper CONTINUOUS FORMS that are folded at the perforations in alternating directions

fatal error an error in a program that causes the termination of execution

father file see GENERATION DATA SET

fault a physical condition that causes a hardware device to fail to operate properly, such as a short circuit

FAX short for **FACS**IMILE **1** the transmission over communication lines of an image, such as a diagram, in the form of electrical signals to another location, where they are reproduced as the original image on special equipment and paper **2** such a reproduction

FDM abbreviation for FREQUENCY–DIVISION MULTIPLEXING

feasibility study a study to determine the benefits and costs, in terms of time, money, and manpower, of a proposed use of a computer to accomplish a given purpose, usually with a recommendation or proposed alternatives

feedback data produced as output by a program and used as input to another phase in the same program, as to modify or correct the factors that have produced the output

fetch **1** to bring an instruction or data into the CPU from main memory **2** the process of doing so **3** loosely, to bring data into main memory from an external storage device

fetch–ahead the process of fetching an instruction before the last instruction has finished executing

fetch cycle **1** the time during which an instruction or data is being fetched **2** INSTRUCTION CYCLE

fiber optics the technology of transmitting data over communication lines made from flexible strands of glass or plastic through which laser beams or light from LEDs are passed to transfer data. The strands are formed into cables and can carry many more times the amount of data than traditional copper wire

Fibonacci number an integer in a Fibonacci series

Fibonacci search a dichotomizing search in which the number of items in a file is either equal to a Fibonacci number or assumed to be equal to the next higher Fibonacci number: in each step in the search, the file (or subset of the file) is divided and the number of remaining items in each of the subsets corresponds to successively smaller numbers in the Fibonacci series

Fibonacci series a series of integers in which each integer is equal to the sum of the preceding two integers, as in 1, 2, 3, 5, 8, 13, 21

field any of the units of storage that are grouped together to form a record: for example, a field might be an individual's age and could be grouped with other related fields concerning one individual

FIFO (FIE foh) acronym for **F**IRST **I**N **F**IRST **O**UT See QUEUE

figurative constant a word in a programming language used to represent a commonly used constant, such as **zero** for 0, in order to make the program easier to write and understand

file a collection of logically related records dealt with as a unit: for example, a payroll file is a collection of employee payroll records See DATA SET

file conversion **1** the process of transferring a file from one type of storage medium to another, as from disk to tape **2** the process of converting a file from one type of data structure to another, as from a sequential file to an indexed sequential file

file directory CATALOG

file gap INTERRECORD GAP

file layout the defined arrangement of records in a file, including their order and the length of the fields and records

file maintenance the addition and deletion of records in a file in order to keep the information current and accurate

file management the development and use of rules and procedures in creating, updating, and retrieving information from a file

file mark a code indicating that the last record in a file has been read

file organization DATA STRUCTURE

file protection the methods by which a file is protected from unauthorized use, such as the use of passwords, or from accidental erasure, such as a file protect ring

file protect ring a plastic ring placed on the back of a magnetic tape when data is to be recorded: when the ring is not in place, the tape drive senses its absence and will not write on the tape, thus protecting against accidental or unauthorized writing. In some systems, when the ring is in place, the tape cannot be written on

file structure DATA STRUCTURE

fill **1** an arbitrary character, such as a blank or a zero, used to complete a field, record, or block **2** to so place characters

filler one or more nondata characters placed in a field so that all positions in the field are occupied, in order to bring it to a standard size

firmware a program stored on a ROM that controls the operation of the computer: firmware is built into the circuitry of a ROM and is opposed to software or programs that can be altered by programmers: for example, calculators contain firmware with the instructions for performing the various mathematical operations

first generation computer a computer of the generation classified as beginning around 1951, characterized by physically large units using vacuum tube circuitry, stored programs, and mostly magnetic tape for auxiliary storage See COMPUTER GENERATIONS

fix PATCH

fixed designating permanence in a type of storage, as in a ROM, a FIXED WORD–LENGTH COMPUTER, or a RESIDENT program

fixed disk a disk or disk pack that is permanently mounted on a disk drive Compare REMOVABLE DISK

fixed–head disk a disk drive in which the read–write heads do not move. Each track has a separate read–write head, thereby decreasing the length of time necessary to read and write data Compare MOVABLE–HEAD DISK

fixed–length records records in a file, each of which has the same number of characters, bits, etc. Compare VARIABLE–LENGTH RECORDS

fixed–point notation the representation of a number where the RADIX POINT is assumed to be in a fixed position, for example, at the extreme left, so that all numbers are dealt with as fractions Compare FLOATING–POINT NOTATION

fixed–point number **1** a number represented in fixed–point notation **2** a number having no RADIX POINT: an integer Compare FLOATING–POINT NUMBER

fixed–point operation an arithmetic operation performed on numbers in FIXED–POINT NOTATION Compare FLOATING–POINT OPERATION

fixed–point part MANTISSA

fixed–point representation the representation of a fixed–point number in a FULL WORD of storage where the leftmost bit indicates the sign (0 for positive, 1 for negative) and the remaining bits represent the value of the number Compare FLOATING–POINT REPRESENTATION

fixed storage READ–ONLY STORAGE

fixed word–length computer a computer in which each machine word always contains the same number of bits: the registers and storage locations are all designed to contain that number of bits. Fixed–word length computers are word–addressable Compare VARIABLE WORD–LENGTH COMPUTER

flag a variable used in a program to indicate whether a condition has or has not occurred: for example, a flag could be used to indicate that a record was found to have an error in one of its fields

flat–bed plotter a plotter in which the paper is held on a flat surface over which a beam supporting a pen moves back and forth to record the data

flexible disk FLOPPY DISK

Flexowriter a trademark for an earlier machine used to produce punched paper tape from data entered on a keyboard

flicker   the rapid fading in and out of images on the screen of a CRT due to a refresh rate that is not high enough to maintain a steady image

flip–flop   a storage unit capable of storing a bit: the flip–flop is a circuit that maintains a value of 1 or 0 until a TRIGGER directs it to change. It is one of the most common circuits in a digital computer

flippy   DOUBLE–SIDED FLOPPY

floating–point notation   the representation of a number as a fraction multiplied by a power of the base: for example, the binary number 10011 (or .10011 x 2^5) would be represented in floating–point notation as .10011E+5, where .10011 is the fractional portion and +5 is the exponent. Such notation allows very large numbers to be stored in a word of a limited number of bits, with some of the bits used for the exponent and the rest for the fraction   Compare FIXED–POINT NOTATION

floating–point number   a number represented in floating–point notation: the position of the radix point moves (or "floats") because all numbers involved in a floating–point operation must have the same exponent   Compare FIXED–POINT NUMBER

floating–point operation   an arithmetic operation performed on floating–point numbers where the radix points are shifted to allow addition of numbers with differing exponents: for example, to add the floating–point decimal numbers .12 x 10^3 and .654 x 10^5, the decimal point in the first number must be shifted to the left two positions so that the exponents of the two numbers are the same. The first number would become .0012 x 10^5 and can now be added to .654 x 10^5 and result in .6552 x 10^5. The computer automatically keeps track of the positions of the radix points, thus making floating–point operations advantageous in calculations involving very large or very small numbers requiring high precision Compare FIXED–POINT OPERATION

floating–point representation the representation of a floating–point number in a FULL WORD or DOUBLE WORD of storage: in a full word of 32 bits, the leftmost bit indicates the sign of the fraction (0 for positive, 1 for negative), the next seven bits represent the exponent, and the fraction is represented by the rightmost 24 bits Compare FIXED–POINT REPRESENTATION

floppy disk a disk, usually 5 1/4 or 8 inches in diameter, made of a flexible piece of Mylar and coated with a material that can be magnetized to store bits: floppy disks are inserted into a small disk drive called a **floppy disk drive** (some systems can use up to four disk drives in series) and can be used to read or write data with any size computer, although they are most commonly used with microcomputers and minicomputers. The 5 1/4–inch disk can store approximately 100,000 bytes (characters) whereas the 8–inch disk can store approximately 300,000 bytes

flowchart a graphic description through the use of FLOWCHART SYMBOLS of the various paths, branches, and decisions within a program or system: flowcharts are used by systems analysts to describe systems **(system flowchart)**. Flowcharts are used by programmers as the first step before writing programs and as a means of communication among several programmers assigned to a single project or system **(program flowchart)** See BLOCK DIAGRAM, LOGIC DIAGRAM, FLOW DIAGRAM

flowchart symbol a symbol, such as a rectangle, circle, etc., used to represent any of the logical steps of a program or system in terms of input/output, storage, and processing of data: for example, the input operation to read data would be represented in a flowchart as a parallelogram appropriately labeled "READ"

flowchart template a plastic or metallic plate that is used in the preparation of a flowchart as a pattern for tracing flowchart symbols

flow diagram a type of flowchart that depicts the details of how an algorithm is used to solve a problem: a flow diagram does not generally represent input/output operations but instead concentrates on the algorithm

flowline the line connecting two flowchart symbols and representing, by the means of arrowheads, the path along which the transfer of data or program control proceeds

FM abbreviation for FREQUENCY MODULATION

font a complete assortment of type characters of a given size and style

forbidden designating an illegal character or operation

foreground the teleprocessing or multiprogramming environment in which higher-priority tasks are processed before those of a lower priority Compare BACKGROUND

foreground program a high-priority program that executes before any programs of a lower priority Compare BACKGROUND PROGRAM

foreign exchange a data communications service offered by telephone companies, providing permanent leased lines between a customer and a location outside the local public telephone system

format the defined arrangement and location of data items within a larger unit of storage: for example, a record contains a specified number of fields occurring in a specified sequence

format effector a CONTROL CHARACTER used to control the format with which data is printed, recorded, or displayed

form feed character a FORMAT EFFECTOR causing a printer to move to the first line on the next page or form

FORTRAN acronym for **FOR**MULA **TRANS**LATOR a high–level programming language that is used to write programs dealing primarily with mathematical formulas and expressions, similar to algebra and used mainly in scientific and technical applications: one of the oldest languages, it is still widely used because of its compact notation, the many subroutines provided to solve mathematical problems, and the ease with which arrays, matrices, and loops can be handled

four–address computer a computer in which each machine instruction contains four addresses: the addresses of both operands, the address of where the result is to be stored, and the address of the next instruction Compare THREE-ADDRESS COMPUTER, TWO–ADDRESS COMPUTER, ONE-ADDRESS COMPUTER See MULTIADDRESS

fourth generation computer a computer generation characterized by physically small, lower-cost microcomputers using microprocessors and memory chips: there is disagreement as to whether this is a new generation or merely an advanced stage of the third generation See COMPUTER GENERATIONS

fox message a sentence typed into a terminal to ensure that data is being transmitted correctly:

usually some form of 'the quick brown fox jumps over the lazy dog', since it contains every letter in the alphabet, followed by each of the numerals

FPLA abbreviation for FIELD PROGRAMMABLE LOGIC ARRAY a PLA that can be programmed by the user

fragmentation in a multiprogramming environment, the occurrence of storage locations in main memory that are not being used by programs but are grouped together in such small numbers that they cannot be used to store pages from other programs

frame **1** PAGE FRAME **2** one row of bit positions across a magnetic or paper tape, usually capable of storing one character **3** in data communications, a group of bits transmitted as a unit

framing the communication process that determines which group of bits constitutes a character and which group of characters represents a MESSAGE: framing is handled by the particular PROTOCOL of the communication system

framing error an error caused by the failure of a receiving device to correctly identify those bits that constitute a character

frequency–division multiplexing in data communications, a multiplexing technique in which a high bandwidth line is divided into several narrow bands of lower frequency, which are used to carry data from a number of terminals simultaneously Compare TIME–DIVISION MULTIPLEXING

frequency loading a technique for storing the most frequently used records at the beginning of a file so as to reduce access time

frequency modulation a MODULATION technique in which the frequency of a signal is altered to differentiate between a binary 1 and 0: a lower frequency is used for 0

front–end processor in a timesharing system, a small computer of limited capability that is programmed to control remote terminals and to perform certain other functions, such as converting data into the necessary codes and formats or correcting errors, thus allowing the host computer to process data without regard for slower input/output operations

full–adder a combinational circuit that performs the arithmetic addition of three bits, two that are significant bits and one that is a carry bit from a previous position Compare HALF–ADDER

full–duplex designating the transmission of data in two directions at the same time, as from a terminal to the computer and from the computer to the terminal Compare SIMPLEX, HALF–DUPLEX

full word a WORD used to store data Compare HALF WORD, DOUBLE WORD

fully formed character a printed character that is a complete image formed by uninterrupted strokes Compare DOT–MATRIX CHARACTER

function a set of ordered pairs of numbers, denoted $y = f(x)$, with the property that any x value uniquely determines a y value: for example, if x is equal to 3 in the function $y = 2x$, then y must equal 6 See LINEAR FUNCTION, NONLINEAR FUNCTION

functional unit any of the various units in a computer system capable of performing the arithmetic, control, storage, input, or output function

function code OP CODE

function key 1 on a keyboard, a key used to perform a function for the operator, such as an ENTER KEY 2 PROGRAM FUNCTION KEY

function program OBJECT PROGRAM

G

gang punch a reproducer or a type of keypunch that punches the value found in one field of a record onto a specified number of succeeding punch cards

gap INTERRECORD GAP

garbage unwanted or meaningless data

garbage collection an automatic procedure that identifies storage locations in main memory that contain data no longer needed by the program currently executing and makes them available for use by other programs

gate a circuit that has one or more input signals and produces a single output of binary 1 or 0, depending on the type of logic built into the circuit: gates are combined to form COMBINATIONAL CIRCUITS or SEQUENTIAL CIRCUITS. Some of the basic gates are the AND GATE, OR GATE, NAND GATE, NOT GATE, XOR GATE, EXCLUSIVE–NOR GATE, and the INVERTER

GE an abbreviation for GREATER THAN OR EQUAL TO, used as a relational operator in a program

generalized routine a routine designed to solve a general class of problems: it is supplied with various parameters when it is used on a specific job within that general class: for example, a generalized sort routine can be used to sort in ascending, descending, or alphabetical order

general–purpose computer a computer designed to perform a wide variety of operations using a wide variety of programming languages: such a computer could be found in a university, where many different types of programs are written for a variety of purposes, such as research by professors, class assignments by students, and registration by the staff   Compare SPECIAL-PURPOSE COMPUTER

general purpose interface the registers or portion of memory available to two or more programs

general purpose interface bus GPIB

general purpose operating system an OPERATING SYSTEM designed to handle a wide variety of operations so that it can be used for different applications without being altered

general-purpose program a program that performs a basic function (or functions) commonly needed in many other programs

general register an addressable register that can be used for any of a variety of functions and is not committed to one specific function

generate to produce new data, a routine, or a program from data and/or specifications that are input to a program

generated address an address of an instruction or data generated during the execution of a program

generation see COMPUTER GENERATIONS

generation data set a collection of a number of versions of a master file retained for a designated number of updates in order to avoid irrecoverable loss of current data: the files are often stored in groups of three, referred to as the **grandfather**, **father**, and **son files**, the last being the most current copy

generator program a program that produces another program or data as output, as, for example, a report generator

get to READ a record

giga– a prefix meaning one billion or 10^9

gigacycle KILOMEGACYCLE

GIGO (GIG oh) acronym for **G**ARBAGE **IN**, **G**ARBAGE **O**UT noting the fact that garbled or incorrect input to a computer results in garbled or incorrect output

glitch a small BUG, especially one caused by a voltage surge or electrical noise that causes an error in the transmission of data

global variable a variable that refers to the same value wherever its name is used in a program Compare LOCAL VARIABLE

GO TO a programming statement designating a branch to another statement in the same program

GP abbreviation for GENERAL PURPOSE

GPIB abbreviation for GENERAL PURPOSE INTERFACE BUS a standard interface for connecting various devices to a microcomputer: it consists of a 24–pin connector

grandfather file see GENERATION DATA SET

graphics COMPUTER GRAPHICS

gray code a binary code in which only one bit position is changed in each successive bit pattern for representing the decimal number: the gray code was developed for input/output devices in order to eliminate the erroneous readings that occur when bit patterns change in more than one position from one decimal number representation to the next

grouping the process of arranging together those records in a file that meet a specified criterion, such as all records for the group of salaried employees

group mark an indicator signaling the end of a unit of data, such as a word, record, or file

GT an abbreviation for GREATER THAN, used as a relational operator in a program

guide edge the edge of a data medium, such as paper or magnetic tape, used to guide it into the tape drive or reader

gulp a group of several bytes treated as a unit

H

half–adder a combinational circuit that performs the arithmetic addition of two bits: the circuit produces the sum bit and a carry bit: for example, the addition of two bits, $1 + 1$, is equal to 10. The half–adder outputs a sum of 0 and a carry of 1 into the next bit position Compare FULL–ADDER

half–duplex designating the transmission of data in only one direction at a time, as from a terminal to the computer or from the computer to the terminal Compare SIMPLEX, FULL–DUPLEX

half word half of a WORD, used to store data that is small enough to be represented in half the number of bits of a word Compare FULL WORD, DOUBLE WORD

halt 1 a termination in the execution of a program caused by an interrupt, error, or instruction 2 such an instruction 3 to so stop the execution of a program

halt instruction an instruction that stops the execution of a program until a specified manual intervention occurs, such as the mounting of a specified magnetic tape

handler a routine responsible for handling input/output operations or for controlling the operation of an input/output device

handshaking the exchange of control characters between an input/output device and an I/O INTERFACE: the characters indicate that the device is ready to receive data, that data has been sent, and that the data has been accepted

hands–on designating an activity or training that involves the actual operation of a piece of hardware, such as a terminal

hard copy computer output that is printed on paper and can be read and handled by people: a hard copy is opposed to other computer output that may be temporarily displayed on a terminal or recorded on another medium, such as a magnetic tape Compare SOFT COPY

hard disk a disk made of a rigid base, such as ceramic or aluminum, coated with a magnetic material: hard disks store approximately 3 to 10 million bytes (or characters) Compare FLOPPY DISK

hard error PERMANENT ERROR

hard–sectored designating a floppy disk in which holes have been punched to mark the boundaries of each SECTOR: space is not needed on the disk for records marking the boundaries Compare SOFT–SECTORED

hardware the physical equipment and components in a computer system Compare SOFTWARE

hardware check **1** AUTOMATIC CHECK **2** a malfunction occurring in a hardware device

hardware monitor a device that collects measurements of electrical events, such as voltage levels or pulses, in a digital computer for the purpose of evaluating its performance: for example, it could be used to measure the amount of time a CPU is idle while input/output operations are being performed Compare SOFTWARE MONITOR

hard-wired **1** designating a terminal that is directly connected to the computer **2** designating a device with permanently wired circuitry enabling it to perform a fixed set of operations

hash GARBAGE

hashing **1** a technique in which a mathematical calculation is applied to the key of a record and the resulting value (called the **hash address** or **hash index**) is the location, such as a track number, on a disk where the record will be stored **2** any technique that transforms one or more fields in a record into a more compact field

hash total a sum obtained by adding the values in a particular field and comparing it to the sum obtained in the same manner at an earlier stage, in order to check for errors: a hash total is often obtained from fields that would not normally be involved in arithmetic operations, such as social security numbers

HDLC abbreviation for HIGH-LEVEL DATA LINK CONTROL a standard BIT-ORIENTED PROTOCOL developed by the International Standards Organization, in which control information is always placed in the same position, and specific bit patterns used for control differ from those used in representing data, so that errors are less likely to occur: ADCCP and SDLC are two similar protocols

head READ-WRITE HEAD

head crash a CRASH caused when a read–write head touches the surface of a disk, generally resulting in permanent damage at the point of impact: read–write heads are normally suspended just above the surface of the disk

header 1 control information, such as source, destination, and priority, prefixed to transmitted data **2** the first record in a file, or first field in a record, containing information to identify the file or record

header label a label record, stored at the beginning of a file on magnetic tape, that contains descriptive information about the file, such as the data set name, density, creation date, retention period, volume number, and generation number of a file Compare TRAILER LABEL

header record HEADER LABEL

heading in data communications, a sequence of communications control characters containing information about the data to be transmitted, such as its destination, that is transmitted following a START OF HEADING character and preceding the TEXT

head–per–track disk FIXED–HEAD DISK

hertz a measure of frequency equal to one cycle per second

heuristic designating a trial and error method, using rules of thumb, for finding the solution to a problem by evaluating the progress made at steps along the way Compare ALGORITHM

hex clipped form of HEXADECIMAL

hexadecimal designating a situation in which there is a choice of sixteen different possible values or states

hexadecimal digit any one of the 16 digits in the hexadecimal number system, represented by 0, 1, 2, 3, 4, 5, 6, 7, 8, 9, A, B, C, D, E, and F

hexadecimal number a number in the hexadecimal number system represented by one or more hexadecimal digits

hexadecimal number system the base 16 number system that represents a hexadecimal number as the sum of successive powers of 16: for example, the hexadecimal number 4AC8 can be expressed as $(4 \times 16^3) + (10 \times 16^2) + (12 \times 16^1) + (8 \times 16^0)$, where $16^0 = 1$, and is equivalent to the decimal number 19,144

hexadecimal point the RADIX POINT in a hexadecimal number that has an integer and fractional part: for example, 4AE.F9

hierarchy a group of hardware or software items arranged according to rank, class, priority, etc.

high–level data link control HDLC

high–level language a programming language, such as BASIC or COBOL, that is not dependent upon the machine language of a computer, requires a compiler to translate it into machine language, and has been designed to allow the use of words similar to those in the English language Compare LOW–LEVEL LANGUAGE

highlight to emphasize part of an image on a CRT by having it blink, underlining it, using REVERSE VIDEO, intensifying it, etc.

high–order bit the bit to the far left in a WORD

high–speed printer a printer whose speed is compatible with the speed of computation so that it can operate on–line, such as a line printer with a speed of at least 600 lines per minute

highway BUS

HIPO (HIGH poh) acronym for **H**IERARCHY OF **I**NPUT, **P**ROCESSING, and **O**UTPUT a chart identifying the input records or data items to a particular processing step in a program, the processing to be accomplished, and the output to be produced

hit **1** in a program, the successful finding of two data items with the same value, as in searching a file for a record that contains a specified key **2** a hardware malfunction

hit–on–the–fly printer a printer in which the paper and/or the printing mechanism are in constant motion so that starts and stops are not needed

hit ratio the ratio of the number of times items of data are successfully located in main memory to the total number of attempts over a given time period

hog a program that requires large amounts, or the exclusive use, of an available resource, such as main memory

holding time the length of time a communication channel is in use for the transmission of one message

Hollerith card 80–COLUMN CARD

Hollerith code a code in which each character is represented by a unique combination of punched holes in a column of an 80–COLUMN CARD: each column has 1 hole punched to represent a number, 2 holes punched to represent a letter, and 3 to 6 holes punched to represent a special symbol. A total of 64 unique characters (10 digits, 26 letters, 27 special symbols, and a blank) are included in the Hollerith code character set. The code is named for the inventor of the PUNCH CARD in 1890, Herman Hollerith (1860–1929)

home address on some disks, a field stored on each track, containing the cylinder number and the number of the read–write head used to access data on that track: blocks of data are written following the home address on the track and are numbered sequentially from that field

home computer PERSONAL COMPUTER

home record the first record in a chain of records See CHAINED FILE

hopper CARD HOPPER

host computer a computer to which a number of terminals and/or other smaller computers are connected and which provides computation, access to stored files, programming languages, and other such services

housekeeping the process of performing various operations prior to and following the execution of a program, such as making available the files needed by the program, setting up the necessary peripheral devices, and cleaning up temporary storage areas when the program has finished executing

HSP abbreviation for HIGH–SPEED PRINTER

human–oriented language a programming language employing words very similar to those used in ordinary speech

hybrid computer a computer that is a combination of an analog and digital computer linked together by an interface system for converting analog data to digital data and vice versa: used in scientific research and other such specialized applications

Hz abbreviation for HERTZ

I

IBG abbreviation for INTERBLOCK GAP

IBM card 80–COLUMN CARD

IC abbreviation for **1** INTEGRATED CIRCUIT **2** INSTRUCTION COUNTER

identifier a label assigned to a device, variable, constant, or the like, that identifies it in a program

idle time the period of time during which the computer is operating correctly but is not in use

IDP abbreviation for INTEGRATED DATA PROCESSING

IEEE (EYE triple E) abbreviation for INSTITUTE OF ELECTRICAL AND ELECTRONICS ENGINEERS a computer society formed to advance computer and data processing technology by promoting cooperation and exchange of information among its members and excellence within the field

IEEE 488 a set of standards adopted by the IEEE: also called GPIB

IFIPS (EYE fips) acronym for INTERNATIONAL FEDERATION OF INFORMATION PROCESSING SOCIETIES a multinational federation of data processing societies to promote and advance international cooperation in the fields of information science and data processing

IF–THEN a programming statement in which a condition is tested and subsequent action is taken when the condition is true: for example, the statement "IF A = B THEN C = 1" tests whether A equals B, and will set C equal to 1 only when that condition is true

IF-THEN-ELSE a programming statement that tests a condition and provides for one action to be taken when the condition is true and another to be taken when it is false: for example, the statement "IF A = B THEN C = 1 ELSE C = 2" will set C equal to 1 when A equals B and will set C equal to 2 when A does not equal B

illegal character an arrangement of bits that is not recognized as a specific character in a given computer

illegal operation an operation, specified in an instruction, that cannot be properly executed because it is not recognized by the computer as a valid operation

IML, IMPL abbreviations for INITIAL MICROCODE (or MICROPROGRAM) LOAD the process of loading a microprogram into main memory, usually from a diskette

immediate addressing an addressing mode in which the data to be processed by the OP code of an instruction is contained within the instruction: the operand contains the data rather than an address where the data is stored

impact printer a printer that operates by striking individual raised characters or wire ends against an inked ribbon and paper: impact printers produce FULLY FORMED CHARACTERS or DOT-MATRIX CHARACTERS, either one character or one line at a time See BAR PRINTER, CHAIN PRINTER, DAISY-WHEEL PRINTER, DRUM PRINTER, THIMBLE PRINTER, TRAIN PRINTER, WIRE-MATRIX PRINTER

imperative statement EXECUTABLE STATEMENT

implied decimal point ASSUMED DECIMAL POINT

incidentals time the amount of time a computer is used for demonstrations, training, and the like

inclusive-OR OR

inclusive–OR gate OR GATE

increment **1** a quantity added to another quantity **2** to add a quantity, usually 1, to another quantity: for example, in order to keep track of the number of times a loop has executed, a counter can be incremented by 1 each time the loop executes. The counter can then be tested to determine whether the loop has executed the desired number of times Compare DECREMENT

incremental compiler a compiler that translates programming statements into machine language as they are typed into a terminal so that the entire program does not have to be recompiled when a new statement is added

index **1** a table containing the keys to the records in a file and the locations where they are stored **2** to prepare such a table **3** SUBSCRIPT

indexed sequential access method an ACCESS METHOD in which an index is stored with a sequential file: the index contains the key for each record in the file and its corresponding location, such as the track number on disk, where it is stored. The index can be used to provide direct access to a file that would otherwise only provide sequential access

indexed sequential file a SEQUENTIAL FILE ordered on the basis of unique record keys: the file has an index stored with it containing addresses or pointers that indicate where each record in the file is located. An indexed sequential file is stored on a DIRECT ACCESS STORAGE DEVICE and may be accessed sequentially or randomly

index hole a hole punched in a floppy disk to mark the beginning of each track on a SOFT-SECTORED disk or to mark the beginning of each sector on a HARD-SECTORED disk

indexing an ADDRESS MODIFICATION technique in which the value stored in the index register is added to the address specified in an instruction in order to determine the address of where the operand is to be stored or retrieved

index mark **1** INDEX HOLE **2** a record placed on a SOFT–SECTORED disk to mark the beginning of a sector

index register a register that is used primarily in ADDRESS MODIFICATION in order to access sequential storage locations in main memory without changing the part of the instruction containing the address: for example, the contents of the index register can be added to the address specified in an instruction. The new address is used to store or retrieve data and the value in the index register is increased by a specified number. When the instruction is again executed, the addition of the contents of the index register causes it to store or retrieve data in the next storage location

indicator **1** a device that indicates some condition in a computer, as a light indicating that a piece of equipment is operating **2** an item of data indicating that a condition, such as an overflow, has occurred during the execution of a program **3** FLAG

indirect addressing an addressing mode in which the ADDRESS PART of an instruction refers to the address of a storage location that holds the address of the operand: indirect addressing is used in assembly language programming to address memory locations outside the range permitted by the instructions

inequality a proposition that states the relationship of two items of data or two mathematical expressions where one is greater or less than the other: used in a program to determine further action, as in "IF A LESS THAN B THEN C = B"

inequivalence XOR

infinite loop a loop that, due to an error in the writing of a program, continues to execute until the operator cancels the program or the time allotted to the program expires and it is terminated

infix notation a notation for an arithmetic expression in which the operators, such as + or –, are written in between the operands: for example, the expression A + B is written in infix notation Compare PREFIX NOTATION, POSTFIX NOTATION

informatics all the technologies, collectively, that deal with the computer–assisted collection, processing, and transmission of information

information data that has been processed by a computer and produced as output in a form meaningful to a user

information bits those bits containing the data to be processed, not including parity bits and other such bits that convey information about the data

information management system a system designed to create, update, and maintain a file or data base

information processing DATA PROCESSING

information retrieval system a system designed to retrieve data from a storage device, usually disk, and display it quickly to the requesting person in the proper form and format

information routing the process of selecting a path for the transmission of data to a specified destination

information science the field of study concerned with the development of techniques and systems for the efficient organization, storage, and dissemination of information

information storage and retrieval the use of a computer system for storing large amounts of related data, items of which can be quickly and easily retrieved and viewed by various people

information system a collection of people, procedures, and equipment maintained to collect, record, process, store, retrieve, and display information

inherited error an error in data caused by a previous error in another step of the program

initialization the process of setting various counters, addresses, or variables in a program to their starting value

initialize to set a storage location, counter, variable, or the like to a beginning value, such as zero, before beginning the routine

initial program load IPL

initiator–terminator a routine in the JOB SCHEDULER that performs the necessary functions in selecting a job to execute, allocating input/output devices, and printing the output

ink–jet printer a NONIMPACT PRINTER that prints DOT–MATRIX CHARACTERS at high speed one at a time by spraying small jets of electrostatically charged ink in patterns guided by a computer program onto ordinary paper

in–line coding see OPEN SUBROUTINE

in–line processing the processing of items of data in the order in which they were input, without prior sorting, editing, or grouping

input 1 designating data and/or programs entered or to be entered into the computer for processing **2** to so enter data and/or programs **3** such data and/or programs Compare OUTPUT

input area INPUT BLOCK

input block a portion of main memory or auxiliary storage used to store programs and data that have been input to the computer system and are waiting to execute

input–bound designating a device that can output data more quickly than the rate at which data is being input to it, as in a computer using paper tape input Compare OUTPUT–BOUND

input device a device that can only input data to the computer, such as a CARD READER

input field UNPROTECTED FIELD

input job queue JOB QUEUE

input job stream JOB STREAM

input mode a mode of operation for a terminal in which a file may be created or added to by the repeated entry of lines of a program or data Compare EDIT MODE, COMMAND MODE

input/output designating the process of entering data into the computer or of transferring data from the computer to a printer, terminal, or storage medium

input/output bandwidth the maximum rate, expressed in bytes per second, at which data can be transferred to or from peripheral devices in a particular system

input/output bus DATA BUS

input/output channel a processor that controls the transfer of data between main memory and a number of input/output devices: the channel executes CHANNEL COMMANDS and frees the CPU to perform other operations until a transfer of data is complete

input/output controller I/O CONTROLLER

input/output control system a collection of system programs that performs input and output operations for a program and maintains information concerning all the files stored in the computer system, thus relieving the programmer of the need to write detailed input/output instructions

input/output device any ON–LINE device used for the input and/or output of data in a computer, such as tape drives, disks, card readers, card punches, printers, terminals, or floppy disks

input/output interface I/O INTERFACE

input/output operation any operation in which data is read from the medium on which it is stored and is then transferred to main memory, or one in which data is transferred from main memory and written on a medium, such as disk or magnetic tape

input/output orders I/O ORDERS

input/output procedure I/O PROCEDURE

input/output processor INPUT/OUTPUT CHANNEL

input/output programming system the INPUT/OUTPUT CONTROL SYSTEM in a minicomputer

input/output system the hardware and software necessary to enter data into a computer system and to transfer it between various input/output devices and main memory

input/output unit INPUT/OUTPUT DEVICE

input queue JOB QUEUE

input stream JOB STREAM

input work queue JOB QUEUE

inquiry a request entered on a terminal for information from a file stored on a disk: the computer immediately extracts the requested information from the file and sends it back to the terminal, where it can be viewed

installation **1** the location where a computer system and/or any of its various components have been installed **2** the process of installing a computer system or any of its various components

in–stream procedure a set of JCL statements that can be brought into the JCL statements of a program with an EXECUTE STATEMENT so that the set does not have to be written every time it is used within the same job

instruction a set of bits or characters specifying an operation to be performed by the computer and identifying the data on which it is to be performed

instruction code a group of bits specifying a particular operation to be performed by a particular computer: it is usually comprised of an OP code and an operand

instruction control unit CONTROL UNIT (sense 1)

instruction counter PROGRAM COUNTER

instruction cycle the sequence of events by which an instruction is fetched, decoded, and executed See EXECUTION CYCLE

instruction format the defined arrangement of an instruction that determines those characters used for the OP code and those for the OPERAND

instruction length the number of words or bytes used to store an instruction in main memory: in most computers, an instruction is one word in length; others allow varying lengths, such as two words

instruction lookahead the process of fetching and decoding one instruction during the execution of another

instruction mix MIX (sense 1)

instruction register a nonaddressable register in the CPU that holds a copy of the instruction being executed

instruction repertoire INSTRUCTION SET

instruction set **1** MACHINE INSTRUCTION SET **2** the set of instructions available in a given programming language

instruction time the amount of time required to perform an instruction cycle

instruction word a WORD containing a machine instruction Compare DATA WORD

integer any number in the set of all positive and negative whole numbers and zero: +6, −234, and 0 are examples of integers

integer programming in OPERATIONS RESEARCH, a class of procedures used for finding the optimal solution to a problem in which all the variables must be integers

integrated circuit a silicon chip containing electrical components, such as transistors, diodes, resistors, and capacitors, interconnected to form an electronic circuit: integrated circuits have replaced the individual circuits used in older computers because they are smaller in size, cost less, require less power, have a higher reliability against failure, reduce the number of external connections, and increase the operating speed

integrated data processing a method of data processing in which the collection and coding of data in machine–readable form is planned to make it available for a number of programs without having to reenter the data or transfer it to another medium: for example, a transaction at a bank is entered on a terminal with the customer's account number and the amount of the transaction. This data is stored on a disk and subsequently used in a program to update the customer's balance, in another program to prepare a report on the daily transactions of the bank, and in a third program to prepare the customer's monthly statement

intelligent terminal **1** a terminal that can perform certain processing functions on data before it is transmitted to the computer, such as performing simple arithmetic operations, editing and/or formatting data, or recording data, as on a tape or disk Compare DUMB TERMINAL **2** PROGRAMMABLE TERMINAL

interaction the process of entering data on a terminal and receiving a response from the computer

interactive CONVERSATIONAL

interactive compiler a compiler in which each statement entered on a terminal is immediately translated into machine language Compare BATCH COMPILER

interactive processing the compiling and executing of each programming statement at the time it is entered on a terminal, allowing the programmer to see results immediately, to correct errors as they occur, and to make changes to the program as it is executing Compare BATCH PROCESSING

interactive programming CONVERSATIONAL PROGRAMMING

interactive system CONVERSATIONAL SYSTEM

interblock gap INTERRECORD GAP

interface **1** the means of interaction between two devices or systems that handle data in different ways, such as in different codes or formats **2** a shared boundary between two devices, systems, or programs, as in the use of the same register or storage locations

interference   noise or other disturbances in the transmission of data that may cause errors or a loss of data

interleave   **1** to alternate the performance of operations between two or more programs   **2** to place in between, as in alternating the selection of data from two or more terminals in order to transmit them as a single unit   See MULTIPLEXING   **3** MEMORY INTERLEAVING

interlock   **1** MUTUAL EXCLUSION   **2** DEADLOCK

intermediate storage   **1** BUFFER   **2** SCRATCHPAD MEMORY

intermittent error   an error that occurs at random and is usually caused by an external condition, such as dust that appears on the surface of a recording medium, and that may disappear when the tape or disk is moved   Compare CONTINUOUS ERROR

internal bus   a bus for transferring data among various registers and between the ALU and control unit

internal cycle time   CYCLE TIME

internally stored program   STORED PROGRAM

internal memory   MAIN MEMORY

internal sort   a sort of items performed in main memory   Compare EXTERNAL SORT

internal storage   MAIN MEMORY

internal timer   a register whose contents are increased at regular intervals in order to measure time and to synchronize events in the computer

International Standards Organization   a voluntary organization formed to provide international standards for data communications

interpreter **1** a program that translates each statement in a source program into machine language, executes it, and repeats the process for each new statement until the entire program has been executed Compare COMPILER **2** a keypunch that prints along the top of a PUNCH CARD the characters corresponding to the holes punched in the card

interrecord gap the space that separates PHYSICAL RECORDS on an external storage device: interrecord gaps signal the beginning and ending of a block of data

interrupt **1** a temporary halt in executing a program, during which control is transferred to the OPERATING SYSTEM: interrupts may be caused by internal conditions, such as a SUPERVISOR CALL, or by external conditions, such as a signal indicating that an input/output device has completed the transfer of data **2** to so halt the execution of a program

interrupt handler a program in the operating system that performs necessary functions when an interrupt occurs, such as preserving the values in various registers and storage locations and transferring control to various routines to service the interrupt

interrupt–service routine INTERRUPT HANDLER

interrupt vector a number of storage locations in main memory for instructions to be used when an interrupt occurs

interval timer REAL–TIME CLOCK

inverted file a data structure in which there is stored with the file an index that contains a list of frequently used descriptive fields and the locations of those records containing a specified field: for example, an entry in the index could contain "salaried" and the location of records for salaried employees

inverter a gate that produces an output binary 1 when the input is a binary 0, and an output 0 when the input is 1

I/O abbreviation for INPUT/OUTPUT

I/O-bound designating a program or computer that is performing more time-consuming input/output operations than quickly executed computations Compare COMPUTE-BOUND, BALANCED SYSTEM

I/O bus DATA BUS

IOC abbreviation for INPUT/OUTPUT CONTROLLER

I/O channel INPUT/OUTPUT CHANNEL

I/O controller a processor that controls the operation of an input/output device allowing it to operate concurrently with the CPU by executing its own set of I/O ORDERS: for example, a printer has an I/O controller to advance the paper, select the characters to be printed, and control the printing of each line

IOCS abbreviation for INPUT/OUTPUT CONTROL SYSTEM

I/O interface any of various devices used to control the transfer of data between the CPU and input/output devices, such as an INPUT/OUTPUT CHANNEL, a DMA, or an I/O CONTROLLER

I/O interrupt an interrupt caused by a signal indicating that an input/output operation has been completed

I/O orders instructions executed by an I/O controller to control the operations of a specific input/output device, as to start and stop a tape drive

I/O port the port through which data is transferred between the CPU and input/output devices

I/O procedure the sequence of instructions needed to perform the transfer of data between the CPU and input/output devices, including input/output instructions performed by the CPU, CHANNEL COMMANDS executed by the input/output channel, and I/O orders executed by the I/O controller

I/O processor INPUT/OUTPUT CHANNEL

IOPS abbreviation for INPUT/OUTPUT PROGRAMMING SYSTEM

IPL abbreviation for INITIAL PROGRAM LOAD or LOADING or LOADER a process, operation, or program that, by means of a computer operator who sets various switches and/or enters several commands, loads the operating system into main memory

IR abbreviation for 1 INSTRUCTION REGISTER 2 INFORMATION RETRIEVAL

IRG abbreviation for INTERRECORD GAP

irrecoverable error ABEND

ISAM (EYE sam) acronym for INDEXED SEQUENTIAL ACCESS METHOD

ISO abbreviation for INTERNATIONAL STANDARDS ORGANIZATION

item a unit of storage within a larger unit, such as a field in a record

iteration 1 the process of repeating the execution of a set of instructions 2 one such repetition

iterative process the process of repeatedly executing a series of instructions, where each repetition comes progressively closer to the desired result, until a specified condition is met

J

JCL abbreviation for JOB CONTROL LANGUAGE the language used to describe the resource requirements of a program to the operating system: JCL is used to identify the programmer for security and accounting purposes, to specify files needed for processing, to indicate required resources, such as input/output devices, language translators, and CPU processing time, and to separate one program from another. JCL is provided by the computer vendor and cannot be used on another vendor's system

job a unit of work for a computer, such as a program or a group of programs and the related data

job card the first JCL statement in a job, identifying the beginning of the job, the user, the job name, and similar information

job control language JCL

job control program a collection of routines that control the flow of a job through a computer system by reading the program into the system, setting up the necessary resources, initiating the execution, and moving the output to a printer

job definition the JCL statements that define a job, such as the JOB STATEMENT, DATA DEFINITION STATEMENT, and EXECUTE STATEMENT

job input stream JOB STREAM

job management the management of jobs in various stages of processing performed by programs in the OPERATING SYSTEM, such as the INITIATOR/ TERMINATOR

job name a unique name assigned to a program to identify it in the computer system: it is specified in the JCL and chosen by the programmer according to conventions specified by the computer center and the operating system

job output stream OUTPUT STREAM

job queue short for INPUT JOB QUEUE a queue used to store programs that have been read into the computer system and are waiting to execute Compare OUTPUT JOB QUEUE

job scheduler a program in the OPERATING SYSTEM that selects the program to be executed next in a sequence based on the priority ranking assigned to the programs, the availability of main memory, and other such rules it has been designed to implement

job statement the JCL statement that marks the beginning of a job and contains such information as the name of the job, the programmer name, and the account number Compare DATA DEFINITION STATEMENT, EXECUTE STATEMENT

job step any of the programs comprising a job: each program is considered one step in a job

job stream 1 the JCL statements, program or programs, and data (if any) that are entered as a unit into the computer system 2 one or more jobs to be submitted to a computer system

joy stick a manual device connected to a terminal, with a control lever that can be moved or tilted in various directions for moving the cursor to any position on the CRT screen: this device is commonly used in computer graphics and many types of computer games

jump BRANCH

junk GARBAGE

justify to place data that is shorter in length than the available field into the rightmost or leftmost position in the field: the remaining positions are usually filled with a blank or other nondata character See RIGHT JUSTIFY, LEFT JUSTIFY

K

K a letter representing the number 1024 (that is, 2^{10}): the number of bytes in the main memory of a computer might be expressd as 64K, meaning 65,536 bytes

k abbreviation for KILO–

Karnaugh map a diagram, used to simplify BOOLEAN FUNCTIONS, that is composed of squares, each representing one combination of the variables in the function: the square is marked with a 1 when the combinations of variables produce a 1 for the value of the function, and a 0 when the value of the function is 0

Kb abbreviation for KILOBIT

KB abbreviation for KILOBYTE

KBS one kilobyte (1024 bytes) per second

Kc abbreviation for KILOCYCLE

kernel NUCLEUS

key **1** a field used to uniquely identify an item, such as the employee number or social security number in a record **2** any of the buttons on a device that are depressed to enter, copy, or print the characters, or one that performs a special function, such as an ENTER KEY **3** to enter data on a terminal

keyboard an arrangement of keys like that on a typewriter, used to enter data manually into a terminal, keypunch, or other such device

keyboard send/receive a teletypewriter that can receive data from the computer and transmit data through the keyboard Compare AUTOMATIC SEND/RECEIVE

key entry designating the manual input of data on a keyboard

keylock a lock on some terminals that prevents them from being used until a key is inserted and turned to the "on" position

keypunch 1 a machine used for punching data onto PUNCH CARDS, one character at a time: the keypunch includes a hopper that holds unpunched cards, a keyboard for entering data, a punching mechanism, a reader that permits duplication of one card's punched holes in the identical columns of the next card, a device that prints the characters corresponding to the holes punched, and a stacker that holds the punched cards See PUNCH CARD 2 to so punch data onto cards

keypunch card PUNCH CARD

key–to–address transformation see HASHING

key–to–disk designating a procedure or system in which data is typed on a keyboard and directly recorded on a disk, usually a floppy disk

key–to–tape designating a procedure or system in which data is typed on a keyboard and directly recorded on a magnetic tape

key verification the process of determining the accuracy of data punched on a punch card through the use of a VERIFIER

keyword 1 a significant word in a title or text, that describes the content of the text 2 a predefined word in a programming language, that has a special meaning or causes a specific operation to be performed when used in a program: for example, GO TO in COBOL

keyword in context KWIC

KHz abbreviation for KILOHERTZ

kilo– a prefix meaning one thousand

kilobit one thousand bits

kilobyte 2¹⁰ (or 1,024) bytes See K

kilocycle KILOHERTZ

kilohertz one thousand cycles per second

kilomegabit one thousand million bits, or one billion bits

kilomegacycle one thousand million cycles, or one billion cycles, per second

kips acronym for **K**ILO **I**NSTRUCTIONS **P**ER **S**ECOND a measure of the number of instructions (stated in thousands) that can be executed per second by a computer

kludge or **kluge** (KLOOJ) any hardware and/or software system that has been temporarily improvised from various mismatched parts and is therefore unreliable: a slang term sometimes used affectionately of such a makeshift

KSR abbreviation for KEYBOARD SEND/RECEIVE

KWIC acronym for **K**EYWORD **I**N **C**ONTEXT a technique of using a computer to select all the significant words in a title and to enter these in an alphabetical index of titles by keyword

L

label 1 in a program, a name that identifies an instruction, a data value, a record, a file, a device, or a storage location **2** to assign such a name

label record a record that contains information about a file stored on magnetic tape See HEADER LABEL, TRAILER LABEL

language PROGRAMMING LANGUAGE

language processor a generalized term for an assembler, compiler, or interpreter

language translator LANGUAGE PROCESSOR

large scale integration LSI

laser acronym for **L**IGHT **A**MPLIFICATION BY **S**TIMULATED **E**MISSION OF **R**ADIATION a device that emits a very intense, narrow beam of light formed of light waves that have been amplified and concentrated

laser printer a NONIMPACT PRINTER that by means of a laser beam forms DOT–MATRIX CHARACTERS on a photoconductor, which are then transferred to paper, one page at a time

latency **1** the amount of time from the initiation of a call for data by the CONTROL UNIT to the start of the transfer of the data **2** ROTATIONAL DELAY

layout FORMAT

layout character FORMAT EFFECTOR

LCD abbreviation for LIQUID CRYSTAL DISPLAY a type of alphanumeric display using a liquid crystal sealed between two pieces of glass and polarizers and activated by an external light source to form the various characters, as on a digital watch

LE an abbreviation for LESS THAN OR EQUAL TO, used as a relational operator in a program

leader **1** a blank section of magnetic or paper tape at the beginning of a reel, by which it is fed into the drive **2** HEADER (sense 2)

leading edge 1 designating a decision as to whether a loop has executed the specified number of times, placed at the beginning of the loop so that the counter is tested before the loop executes **2** the portion of a pulse during its transition from binary 0 to 1 Compare TRAILING EDGE

leading zeros zeros that precede a number in a storage location, such as "000489"

leased line a permanent communication line between a computer and a terminal, that provides private, full–time access to the connection by a subscriber for a fixed fee Compare DIAL–UP LINE

least significant bit the bit of a binary number that contributes the smallest quantity to the value of that number: for example, in the binary number 1011, the rightmost 1 is the least significant bit Compare MOST SIGNIFICANT BIT

least significant digit the digit of a number that contributes the smallest quantity to the value of that number: for example, in the number 123, the least significant digit is 3 Compare MOST SIGNIFICANT DIGIT

LED abbreviation for LIGHT EMITTING DIODE a semiconductor diode that emits light when a current is passed through it and is used for alphanumeric displays on calculators and the like

left justify to place data in the leftmost positions of a field so that the characters are aligned to a leftmost column position when printed Compare RIGHT JUSTIFY

left shift a shift that moves each bit in a register a specified number of positions to the left

length the number of bits or bytes (characters) in a computer word, field, record, etc.

letter–quality designating printed output from a computer that appears to have been typewritten

lexical analysis the process performed by a compiler in order to identify the various components of a programming statement Compare SYNTACTICAL ANALYSIS

librarian 1 a program that keeps track of and maintains the list of files stored in a library 2 a person who maintains the collection of files stored in a computer system, especially those stored on magnetic tapes

library 1 a stored collection of tested programs, routines, and/or subroutines that have usually been translated into machine language and are available for use by a wide variety of other programs 2 a room where magnetic tapes are kept

LIFO (LIE foh) acronym for LAST IN FIRST OUT See STACK

light emitting diode LED

light pen a hand–held stylus connected by a cable to some CRTs, that can sense the light from a position on the screen and convert it into an electrical signal transmitted to the computer: it can be used to move or delete images on the screen or to create new images

limit check a test performed on various numeric fields in a record to determine if they fall within prescribed limits

line COMMUNICATION LINE

linear function a FUNCTION of the general form $y = a + bx$, where a and b are real numbers and x and y are variables: for example, $y = -3.5 + 6x$. The graph of a linear function is always a straight line

linear optimization LINEAR PROGRAMMING

linear programming a series of techniques in OPERATIONS RESEARCH to find an optimum minimum or maximum solution to a linear function given certain restrictions: a typical linear programming problem might be to find the combination of foods that will satisfy the minimum daily requirement of vitamins and entail the least cost

line control the communication process of determining which location is the transmitting station and which location is the receiving station: line control is handled by the particular PROTOCOL of the communication system

line–discipline DATA LINK CONTROL

line driver BUS DRIVER

line feed the movement of the printing mechanism to the next line on a printer or on a terminal that uses paper instead of a CRT for viewing

line hit a disturbance of the signal causing an error in data transmitted over a communication line

line noise NOISE

line number a number assigned to each statement in a program

line printer a high–speed printer that prints an entire line at one time, usually between 120 and 144 characters, on a continuous, perforated strip of paper with holes along the sides that fit over sprockets to keep the paper aligned See BAR PRINTER, CHAIN PRINTER, DRUM PRINTER, TRAIN PRINTER Compare PAGE PRINTER, CHARACTER PRINTER

line speed the rate at which data can be transmitted over a communication line, expressed in bits per second or as a baud rate

link 1 the hardware and/or software used to connect two or more devices or systems **2** to so connect two or more routines, systems, or devices **3** POINTER

linkage the sequence of control and the transfer of data between various routines in a program or between various devices in a computer system

linkage editor a system program that combines into a module a number of program segments that have been separately assembled or compiled, searches libraries to add needed program segments to the main module, links the segments together so that they can refer to one another, and produces a single program in binary code, called a LOAD MODULE, that can be stored in a library or input to a loader for execution

link–attached REMOTE

linked list a LIST in which each item includes a forward pointer that indicates the location of the next item in the list: the pointer eliminates the need to have the items stored in contiguous locations in main memory or on a DIRECT ACCESS STORAGE DEVICE. A doubly linked list has a forward and backward pointer included with each item

linking loader a loader that combines the functions of a LINKAGE EDITOR and a RELOCATING LOADER into one step: a linkage loader performs the function of a linkage editor on an object program, relocates the object code, and brings it into main memory for execution

liquid crystal display LCD

LISP acronym for **LIS**T **P**ROCESSING a high–level programming language used primarily for list processing, symbol manipulation, and recursive operations: it can handle many different data types, treat programs as data, and provide for the self–modification of the program as it is executing: generally considered a difficult language to learn

list 1 a data structure in which records are stored in an ordered sequence in consecutive locations in main memory or on a DIRECT ACCESS STORAGE DEVICE **2** to print the contents of a file or a program

listing a printed copy of a program or file in human–readable form

list processing language a programming language designed to process data stored in a list by providing easy methods for storing the list, inserting and deleting items, locating items in the list, and other such functions: especially useful for data having a variable structure, as in human languages See LISP

literal an alphanumeric value defined as a constant in a program, usually surrounded by single quotes, such as PRINT 'SUBTOTAL,' where 'SUBTOTAL' is the literal

liveware slang for computer personnel, who deal with hardware and software

load 1 to transfer a program and/or data into main memory from an auxiliary storage device, such as a disk **2** to enter data into a storage device

load–and–go see COMPILE–AND–GO

loader a system program that brings an object program stored on an auxiliary storage device into main memory for execution See ABSOLUTE LOADER, RELOCATING LOADER, LINKING LOADER, BOOTSTRAP LOADER, RESIDENT LOADER

load module 1 the output program from a LINKAGE EDITOR that is in binary code **2** a program that is ready to input to a loader

load point a light–reflective marker indicating the beginning of the usable portion of a magnetic tape

local   designating devices that are directly connected to the computer through an INPUT/OUTPUT CHANNEL and are physically located near the computer   Compare REMOTE

local register   GENERAL REGISTER

local storage   the collection of general registers in a computer that are readily available to the CPU

local terminal   a terminal that is on the same site as the central computer and so can be directly connected to it   Compare REMOTE TERMINAL

local variable   a variable that has a certain value within a given subroutine or macro: another variable with the same name may appear in the same program, but it will refer to a different value   Compare GLOBAL VARIABLE

location   STORAGE LOCATION

lock   a KEY or other group of characters that allows access to specified storage locations or software systems

locked up   **1** designating a processor that is locked out of a shared resource   **2** designating a terminal that cannot accept commands because of an error in the entering of a previous command or because of a malfunction in the terminal

lock out   to prevent a processor from accessing a shared resource, such as main memory, when it is being accessed by another processor so that data cannot be altered by two processors at the same time

logical   **1** designating that which is necessary or to be expected because of what has gone before   **2** having to do with COMPUTER LOGIC   **3** designating the way in which a data structure, hardware device, software system, etc., is perceived by a person, that may differ from its actual functioning or form, as when VIRTUAL STORAGE makes a computer appear to have a larger main memory than it actually has

logical add an OR operation

logical comparison the comparison of two items of data or expressions to determine whether they are the same or different

logical multiply an AND operation

logical operation a nonarithmetic operation performed on bits according to the rules of symbolic logic See AND, NOR, OR, NOT, NAND, XOR

logical operator 1 any of the operators, such as AND, OR, or NOT, used to connect two propositions in a conditional statement **2** any of the operators used in symbolic logic to define the action to be performed See AND, OR, NOT, XOR, NAND, NOR

logical record a record whose size is determined by the kind of data it contains rather than by the size of the storage device in which it is to be held: a physical record may contain one or more logical records

logical shift a SHIFT in which a zero is shifted into one end of a register and the bit at the opposite end is shifted out Compare CIRCULAR SHIFT

logical unit an input/output device identified in a program by a label or number that corresponds to the actual label or number assigned to it: used to allow a change of devices for reading or writing data without having to alter the program Compare PHYSICAL UNIT

logic analyzer an instrument used in hardware testing and debugging, that displays the digital signals being transmitted, usually in binary or hexadecimal notation

logic array an integrated circuit composed of an array of gates that are interconnected as specified by the customer for performing various functions in a computer See PLA

logic circuit GATE

logic device a circuit that performs a logical operation in the computer, such as a GATE, COMBINATIONAL CIRCUIT, or SEQUENTIAL CIRCUIT

logic diagram **1** a graphic representation of the logic devices in a computer, such as flip–flops, gates, and circuits: lines, triangles, small circles, and various other symbols are used to show the basic flow of data through the logic device **2** loosely, FLOWCHART Compare BLOCK DIAGRAM

logic element GATE

logic gate GATE

logic symbol a symbol used to represent a LOGICAL OPERATOR: for example, the symbols ¬, &, and | are used in some high–level languages to represent the logical operators NOT, AND, and OR

log in LOG ON

log off to enter the necessary information to end a session on a terminal Compare LOG ON

log on to enter the necessary information, such as an identification number and/or password, to begin a session on a terminal Compare LOG OFF

longitudinal redundancy check LRC

long precision DOUBLE PRECISION

lookahead the process of anticipating an event and preparing for its occurrence in order to increase the operating speed of the computer, as in bringing a block of records into main memory before they are needed by the program See INSTRUCTION LOOKAHEAD

loop **1** a sequence of instructions in a program that are repeatedly executed until either a predetermined number of repetitions has been completed or a specified condition has been met, as, for example, until variable x is less than variable y **2** to so execute a sequence of instructions

loop counter a counter that is increased or decreased by a number (usually 1) each time a loop is executed, in order to keep track of the number of executions

loop network RING NETWORK

low–level language a programming language, using symbolic code, that is based on the machine language of a particular computer and requires an assembler to translate it into actual machine language Compare HIGH–LEVEL LANGUAGE

low–order bit the bit to the far right in a WORD

LP abbreviation for LINEAR PROGRAMMING

lpm abbreviation for LINES PER MINUTE

lps abbreviation for LINES PER SECOND

LRC abbreviation for LONGITUDINAL REDUNDANCY CHECK a parity check on the bits that are in the same position in each of a sequence of characters, as on the first bit of each character Compare VRC, CRC

LSB abbreviation for LEAST SIGNIFICANT BIT

LSD abbreviation for LEAST SIGNIFICANT DIGIT

LSI abbreviation for LARGE SCALE INTEGRATION the technology that allows the construction of chips comprising many hundreds of thousands of gates: such chips are used in main memories, calculators, and microprocessors Compare SSI, MSI, VLSI

LT an abbreviation for LESS THAN, used as a relational operator in a program

M

machine COMPUTER

machine address ABSOLUTE ADDRESS

machine check interrupt an interrupt caused by a malfunction in equipment

machine code the basic bit patterns a computer is designed to recognize as instructions and data, such as EBCDIC

machine cycle 1 the time it takes to perform one machine operation, such as fetching (or executing) an instruction, or reading data from or writing data in a storage location 2 INSTRUCTION CYCLE

machine error an error in a program caused by a malfunction in the computer or its related equipment

machine instruction an instruction in machine language that the computer can read and directly execute

machine instruction set the set of machine instructions available on a given computer and supplied by the manufacturer

machine language 1 the programming language comprised of a set of unique machine codes that can be directly executed by a given computer: each computer has its own machine language. Programmers rarely use machine languages today because instructions and data must be in binary notation. High-level languages, such as COBOL, are preferred since they can be easily translated into machine language by a compiler 2 loosely, ASSEMBLY LANGUAGE

machine learning the process by which a computer may improve its performance based on prior executions of the same program Compare ARTIFICIAL INTELLIGENCE

machine operation the electronic action in the computer resulting from an instruction

machine operator COMPUTER OPERATOR

machine–oriented language a programming language that corresponds closely to the machine language of a computer, such as an assembly language Compare PROBLEM–ORIENTED LANGUAGE, PROCEDURE–ORIENTED LANGUAGE

machine–readable designating data that has been recorded in such a way, as on punched cards or magnetic tape, that it can be directly read or sensed by the computer

machine word WORD

macro clipped form of MACROINSTRUCTION a single instruction that represents a given sequence of instructions: the macro is defined at the beginning of a program to represent a set of instructions. It can then be used throughout the rest of the program every time that set of instructions is needed

macro assembler an assembler that has the ability to translate macros into machine code: a macro assembler has a MACRO PROCESSOR that expands the macros before the program is assembled

macro call MACRO

macro definition a set of instructions that gives a name to a macro and identifies the sequence of instructions it is to represent in a program

macro generator MACRO PROCESSOR

macroinstruction MACRO

macro library a library that contains one or more macro definitions: commonly used macros are stored in a macro library so that any number of programs can use them

macro processor a program that scans a source program and replaces each macro with the sequence of instructions it represents: this process is called **macro expansion** and is performed before a program is compiled or assembled

mag clipped form of MAGNETIC

magnetic bubble memory BUBBLE MEMORY

magnetic card a storage medium consisting of a rectangular piece of plastic coated with material capable of being magnetized to store bits in a number of channels on its surface: magnetic cards can be grouped together and stored in a cartridge that is mounted on a drive. Each card is automatically withdrawn from the cartridge and placed on a rotating drum that carries it to the read–write heads

magnetic character a character that has been imprinted on a form in magnetic ink See MICR

magnetic core the basic component of core memory, that is made from a magnetic material, such as a nickel–iron metal alloy, and shaped like a doughnut: two wires intersect at its center and are used for polarizing the core in either of two directions to store a bit

magnetic core memory CORE MEMORY

magnetic core storage CORE MEMORY

magnetic disk DISK

magnetic drum a DIRECT ACCESS STORAGE DEVICE that is cylindrical in shape and coated with a material capable of being magnetized to store bits in circular tracks on its surface: a read–write head is positioned on an access arm above each

track. The drum is permanently mounted in a
drive that rapidly rotates it under the access arm.
Magnetic drums hold considerably less data than
disks or magnetic tapes and are less commonly
used, although they provide more rapid access
to data

magnetic ink ink containing magnetic particles
that can be sensed by MICR equipment

magnetic ink character recognition MICR

magnetic tape a storage device made of Mylar
tape, approximately one half inch in width and of
various lengths, such as 800, 1200, or 2400
feet, coated with a material that can be magnetized to store data: seven or nine tracks run the
length of the tape. A row of bits, one in each
track across the width of the tape, is a binary
code in ASCII, BCD, or EBCDIC for a number,
character, or special symbol: for example, a
nine–track tape accommodates the eight–bit
code in EBCDIC and one parity bit; a **seven–track
tape** accommodates the 6–bit code in ASCII or
BCD and a parity bit. The bits are stored in either
200, 556, 800, 1600, or 6250 bits per inch
and are read from the tape into the computer by
a magnetic tape drive. Data on such a tape cannot be accessed directly, but only in sequence

magnetic tape code the code, such as ASCII,
BCD, or EBCDIC, that is used to read or write
data on a magnetic tape

magnetic tape drive a drive on which a tape reel
is placed: the magnetic tape is automatically fed
into a slot, passed over the read–write head, and
wound onto another, permanently mounted reel
to hold the tape while it is being used. The tape
drive reads data by sensing the magnetized
spots on the tape and writes data by placing
magnetized spots (bits) on the tape. This is done

at very high speeds, commonly 100,000 to 300,000 characters per second

magnetic tape label TAPE LABEL

magnetic thin film see THIN–FILM MEMORY

mainframe a CPU or, more precisely, the piece of equipment that contains the CPU: applied chiefly to a larger computer as distinguished from a minicomputer or microcomputer. Mainframe computers most commonly have a word length of 32 bits and operate at speeds 100 to 1000 times faster than smaller computers. They have a memory capacity ranging from approximately 512K to 16 megabytes and are used where large volumes of data are processed, as in large corporations, universities, and government offices

main memory storage located in the computer for programs, along with their data, while they are executing: it is composed of a number of locations, each of which has a unique address and is capable of storing a specified number of bits, such as a byte or a word. It is a read–write memory allowing random access. The storage capacity of a main memory varies among computers See CORE MEMORY, SEMICONDUCTOR MEMORY, BUBBLE MEMORY, CHIP, THIN–FILM MEMORY Compare AUXILIARY STORAGE

main program the program from which a subroutine has been called and to which control is returned after the subroutine has executed

main storage MAIN MEMORY

maintenance programmer a programmer who makes alterations, corrections, and adjustments to existing programs

major sort the controlling field that determines the overall order in which a group of items is sorted Compare MINOR SORT

malfunction a failure in a piece of hardware causing it to operate incorrectly Compare ERROR, MISTAKE

management information system MIS

mantissa 1 the fractional portion of a number in FLOATING-POINT NOTATION 2 the nonnegative, fractional portion of the representation of a logarithm: for example, in the representation of $LOG_{10}42.5 = 1.6284$, .6284 is the mantissa and 1 is the CHARACTERISTIC. Similarly, in $LOG_{10}425 = 2.6284$, .6284 is still the mantissa and 2 is the characteristic

map to establish a correspondence between items, as in MEMORY MAPPING

MAR abbreviation for MEMORY ADDRESS REGISTER

mark a character that indicates the beginning or end of a data item, field, file, record, or block, such as a FILE MARK

mark condition in data communications, the binary 1 condition or state of an electrical current Compare SPACE CONDITION

mark sensing the reading of pencil marks on specialized forms performed by an optical mark reader

mask 1 a WORD containing a selected pattern of bits so that when used with a particular operation it will extract specified bits and suppress others from another word: for example, the bit pattern "00111100" can be used with an AND operation to select the middle four bits of another word 2 to so select bits 3 in the production of a ROM, a photographic stencil of the desired circuit elements 4 in the production of integrated circuits, a photographic stencil of the desired patterns of circuits

masking the process of selecting a desired set of bits from a word by using an instruction that masks, or eliminates, the other bits

massage to manipulate input data to produce output in the desired format

mass storage an external storage device capable of storing large amounts of data See MAGNETIC TAPE, MAGNETIC DRUM, DIRECT ACCESS STORAGE DEVICE

master a device that controls the operation of one or more other devices, as in a MASTER–SLAVE SYSTEM

master console in a computer system with more than one console, the primary console used to transfer information to and from the OPERATING SYSTEM

master control program OPERATING SYSTEM

master file a more or less permanent file containing current information about a subject, such as a payroll, inventory, or accounts receivable, that can be periodically updated by a TRANSACTION FILE: for example, a payroll master file would contain employees' names, addresses, numbers, rates of pay, and year–to–date gross salaries, taxes, and deductions. Each payday, the master file would be updated to reflect the new year-to–date figures and any changes occurring in an employee's record

master mode PRIVILEGED MODE

master–slave system the use of two or more computers that share main memory to process data: one is called the master and has all of the peripheral devices connected to it; the others, called slaves, cannot initiate input/output operations or respond to interrupts signaling the transfer of data, thereby allowing them to rapidly process data while the master handles the system functions

match 1 the process of identifying two or more records stored in one or more files, that have the same key or value in a specified field **2** to so identify records

mathematical programming a series of techniques used in OPERATIONS RESEARCH to find an optimum solution to functions that may be linear or nonlinear, by calculating the maximum (or minimum) value of the function subject to certain restrictions See LINEAR PROGRAMMING

matrix an arrangement of numbers in a rectangular grid, that can be manipulated by mathematical operations such as addition, subtraction, and multiplication: each number in the matrix is uniquely identified by two subscripts, the first indicating the row, the second the column Compare VECTOR

matrix printer WIRE–MATRIX PRINTER

Mb abbreviation for MEGABIT

MB abbreviation for MEGABYTE

Mc abbreviation for MEGACYCLE See MEGAHERTZ

MDR abbreviation for MEMORY DATA REGISTER

mean time between failures a measure of the reliability of a piece of equipment specified by the average time it continues to function without a failure

medium scale integration MSI

mega– a prefix meaning one million

megabit one million bits

megabyte one million bytes

megacycle MEGAHERTZ

megahertz one million cycles per second

member one file stored in a library or partitioned data set

memory a device that can store data recorded in it and from which the data can be retrieved: usually refers to the MAIN MEMORY of a computer See STORAGE

memory address register a nonaddressable register in the CPU containing an address of a location in main memory for storing and retrieving instructions and data

memory address space the range of addressable storage locations in a main memory

memory allocation STORAGE ALLOCATION

memory bandwidth the maximum rate, expressed in bytes per second, at which data can be transferred to or from main memory in a particular computer system

memory bank a RAM consisting of a number of contiguous storage locations: used in a computer with other banks containing a similar number of locations

memory cell a unit of storage in main memory that is capable of storing one bit

memory cycle **1** the steps involved in reading data from or writing data in main memory **2** the amount of time needed to read or write data from or in main memory: such time is measured in nanoseconds or microseconds

memory data register a nonaddressable register in the CPU that stores data being transferred between the CPU and main memory

memory–dependent designating a program that must be stored in specified storage locations in main memory in order for it to execute correctly Compare RELOCATABLE

memory dump DUMP (sense 1)

memory hierarchy the hierarchy of storage within a computer system arranged according to size, access time, and cost of use, as in one consisting of a small, but rapidly accessed main memory, larger but slower disks, and very large, but slow tape

memory interleaving a method used in computer systems that permits overlapped accesses to two or more memory modules, thus increasing the maximum rate at which data can be transferred between the CPU and main memory: for example, if one memory module contains all the odd numbered addresses and another all the even addresses, they can be accessed simultaneously in order to transfer data to and from sequential storage locations

memory location STORAGE LOCATION

memory–mapped I/O a technique in which specific storage locations in main memory are allotted to input/output devices so that the devices are addressed in the same way as data may be in any other location, thereby eliminating many of the input/output instructions required

memory mapping a method of converting a VIRTUAL ADDRESS to a REAL ADDRESS according to predefined algorithms

memory module an individual circuit board containing 4 or more K of main memory

memory port the connection between main memory and the CPU, through which data is transferred

memory protection a method for avoiding accidental or unauthorized changes in a program by preventing other programs from accessing its storage locations in main memory

memory register MEMORY DATA REGISTER

menu a displayed list of the various functions a person can select to perform on a terminal

merge **1** the process of combining two or more ordered files into one similarly ordered file **2** to so combine files

message in data communications, an item of data with a specific meaning, transmitted over communication lines and composed of a header, the information to be conveyed, and an end–of–message indicator

message switching in data communications, a technique by which the computer collects data from and distributes data to various terminals or computers in the system: the destination of the data is indicated by an address contained in it. The data is stored until the terminal or computer is ready to receive it Compare CIRCUIT SWITCHING, PACKET SWITCHING

mflops (EM flops) acronym for **MI**LLION **FL**OATING–POINT **O**PERATIONS **P**ER **S**ECOND a measure of computing power: usually associated with large computers

MHz abbreviation for MEGAHERTZ

MICR abbreviation for MAGNETIC INK CHARACTER RECOGNITION the reading of characters (printed in magnetic ink) by a machine that records the data on a storage device, such as a magnetic tape or disk: MICR is commonly used in bank computer systems, where magnetic ink characters are printed on checks and deposit slips to represent customer account numbers and other such control information

micro– a prefix meaning one millionth

micro clipped form of MICROCOMPUTER

microcode 1 microinstructions stored in a control memory, such as a ROM, to control the operation of a computer, as opposed to having the same operations carried out by permanently wired circuitry **2** all or part of a microprogram **3** to write all or part of a microprogram

microcomputer a small, low-cost computer containing a microprocessor: it has a random-access memory (RAM) for storing programs during their execution and, commonly, a read-only memory (ROM) for permanent storage of required programs, such as language processors. Microcomputers have a word length of 4, 8, 12, or 16 bits, with 8 and 16 being the most popular, and a memory size ranging generally from 4K to 64K. They are used for a wide variety of purposes, as in small businesses, in small departments within large businesses, and in the home, as for household management, video games, etc. See COMPUTER

microfiche a small sheet of microfilm on which hundreds of pages of greatly reduced copy can be recorded: a special viewer enlarges the copy so that it can be read. A viewer can hold about 750 microfiches, any one of which can be displayed in a very few seconds

microfilm film on which documents, such as computer output, are photographed in a reduced size for convenience in storage and transportation: enlarged prints can be made from such films, or the film can be viewed by projection

microinstruction an instruction that activates specific circuits in the computer to perform part of the operation specified by a machine instruction

microprocessor a chip that contains the ALU, SCRATCHPAD MEMORY, and CONTROL UNIT in a microcomputer: the microprocessor is the CPU of a microcomputer

microprogram a set of microinstructions that control the sequence in which various circuits in the computer are activated in order to execute machine instructions: a microprogram is stored in a control memory that cannot normally be accessed by a programmer but is used by the CPU: for example, if a machine instruction is decoded by the control unit of the CPU specifying the multiplication of two numbers, the proper microprogram is executed to control the sequence of minute operations to be performed by the circuitry in order to multiply those numbers

microprogrammed designating a computer in which the control unit in a CPU activates the various circuits through microinstructions stored in a control memory, rather than through permanently wired circuitry

microsecond one–millionth of a second

migration 1 the process of moving infrequently used data from an on–line storage device to a less expensive, off–line device 2 the process of moving data from an off–line storage device to an on–line device when it is going to be used with greater frequency

milli– a prefix meaning one thousandth

millimicrosecond PICOSECOND

mini clipped form of MINICOMPUTER

minicomputer an intermediate–sized computer that has a word length of 8, 12, 16, 18, 24, or, most commonly, 32 bits and a memory size ranging from approximately 4K to 256K: it generally operates at about twice the speed of a microcomputer and supports many high–level programming languages, such as COBOL and FORTRAN. The largest uses are in process control systems and small business computer systems See COMPUTER

mini floppy a FLOPPY DISK 5 1/4 inches in diameter and capable of storing approximately 100,000 characters

miniperipheral any of various peripheral devices designed for use with a minicomputer, such as a printer, floppy disk drive, CRT, and the like

minor sort the field that determines the order in which a group of items within a larger group will be sorted: for example, a file could be sorted by department number as the major sort, and by last name within each department as the minor sort Compare MAJOR SORT

mips acronym for MILLION INSTRUCTIONS PER SECOND a measure of the number of instructions a computer can perform in a second based on a given mix: the "s" is often dropped from the term, as in referring to a **2 mip computer**

MIS abbreviation for MANAGEMENT INFORMATION SYSTEM an INFORMATION SYSTEM designed to provide to all levels of management the information used to assist in decision–making: the system should provide for quick retrieval of data, hold comprehensive files, be able to answer questions about the data, and present the data in a form that has meaning for the decision maker

miscellaneous time INCIDENTALS TIME

mistake an incorrect use of logic or syntax in a program Compare ERROR, MALFUNCTION

mix **1** a group of varying amounts of different types of instructions used to test the processing speed of a computer **2** in a multiprogramming environment, the different types of jobs that are executed concurrently

mixed number a number having an integer and fractional part: for example, 10.25

mnemonic in a programming language, designating an easily remembered term or abbreviation for any of various instructions and operations, such as STO for "store"

mode a method or condition of operation

modem (MOH dem) acronym for **MO**DULATOR–**DEM**ODULATOR a device that converts digital data output from another device, such as a computer or a terminal, into analog data that can be transmitted over communication lines: it also converts analog data into digital data that can be accepted by another device, such as a computer or a terminal

modular programming an approach to programming in which logical operations, or small groups of related logical operations, are developed and written separately and then later joined to form the program

modulation the process of converting digital data to analog data by adjusting the amplitude, frequency, or phase of a CARRIER in order to transmit the data See MODEM

modulator–demodulator MODEM

module 1 in a program, a sequence of instructions for performing a given task, such as reading the records from a file **2** a plug–in unit of hardware, such as a MEMORY MODULE

modulo a mathematical operation in which a remainder results from division by a specified number: for example, 32 modulo 6 is 2, where

32 is the dividend, 6 is the divisor, and 2 is the remainder

monadic operation an operation involving only one operand: for example, −A is a monadic operation (negation) involving one operand, A, which is preceded by the monadic operator for negative, −

monadic operator an arithmetic operator that involves only one operand: the valid monadic operators are + for positive and − for negative

monitor 1 SUPERVISOR **2** to perform the functions of a supervisor **3** the screen of a CRT, especially one used with a microcomputer

monolithic designating a chip that contains the CPU, memory, and input/output circuits, as distinguished from a chip containing only the CPU

Monte Carlo method in applied mathematics, a method for obtaining an approximate solution to a numerical problem by means of repeated trial-and-error experiments with random numbers

MOSFET acronym for METAL OXIDE SEMICONDUCTOR FIELD EFFECT TRANSISTOR designating integrated circuits used in the manufacture of microprocessors, RAMs, and ROMs, in which **field effect transistors,** that require only a single pole and one current carrier, are used: such circuits are of a higher current density but lower speed than BIPOLAR circuits

most significant bit the bit of a binary number that contributes the largest quantity to the value of that number: for example, in the binary number 1011, the leftmost 1 is the most significant bit Compare LEAST SIGNIFICANT BIT

most significant digit the digit of a number that contributes the largest quantity to the value of that number: for example, in the number 123,

the most significant digit is 1 Compare LEAST
SIGNIFICANT DIGIT

motherboard the main board in a computer, into
which the circuits are plugged

mouse **1** a small, hand–held device that can be
moved over the surface of a tablet, causing the
cursor to move to a corresponding point on the
screen of a CRT: used as for plotting coordinates
in computer graphics **2** a small, hand–held device that is connected to a CRT and used to
enter commands: the mouse is moved on the
surface of a table or the like to position an arrow
on the screen next to the command the user
wishes to enter. Once the arrow is in position, a
button on the top of the mouse is depressed and
the command is executed

movable–head disk a disk drive in which a single
read–write head is used to access the tracks on
the surface of a disk: the head moves to the
specified track, which must then be read or written sequentially Compare FIXED–HEAD DISK

move to copy the data from one storage location
in main memory to another

MPU abbreviation for MICROPROCESSOR UNIT
See MICROPROCESSOR

MSB abbreviation for MOST SIGNIFICANT BIT

MSD abbreviation for MOST SIGNIFICANT DIGIT

msi abbreviation for MEDIUM SCALE INTEGRATION
the amount of integration on a chip comprising
an intermediate number of gates, generally a few
hundred or less: such chips are used in registers,
decoders, and counters Compare SSI, LSI, VLSI

MTBF abbreviation for MEAN TIME BETWEEN
FAILURES

multiaddress designating a computer in which
each machine instruction contains more than

one address: the number of addresses depends on the type of computer See ONE–ADDRESS COMPUTER, TWO–ADDRESS COMPUTER, THREE–ADDRESS COMPUTER, FOUR–ADDRESS COMPUTER

multicomputer system a computer system in which two or more computers are operated by the same computer center to perform independent tasks

multidrop line a communication line that connects a computer and a number of terminals Compare POINT–TO–POINT LINE

multifile volume a tape reel on which a number of different files have been stored

multipass sort EXTERNAL SORT

multiplexer, multiplexor a device used for multiplexing Compare DEMULTIPLEXER

multiplexer (or multiplexor) channel a channel between main memory and a number of input/output devices that allows these devices to operate simultaneously by interleaving the data being transferred: low–speed input/output devices, such as card readers or line printers, are usually connected to multiplexer channels Compare SELECTOR CHANNEL

multiplexing the process of using a single device to simultaneously nandle several similar, but separate, devices or operations by alternating its attention among them, as in a multiprogramming environment where the CPU alternates the execution of programs

multiplex mode BYTE MODE

multipoint line MULTIDROP LINE

multiprocessing system MULTIPROCESSOR

multiprocessor a computer system that has two or more CPUs sharing main memory and input/output devices so that tasks to be performed can be divided among them in order to improve the performance of the system

multiprogramming system a computer system in which two or more programs are executed concurrently by one computer: each program is executed for a given period of time and is then interrupted until its turn to execute again Compare UNIPROGRAMMING SYSTEM

multitasking the technique of concurrently executing a number of related tasks in the same partition, each of which has been assigned a priority and can be interrupted to allow one of the tasks with a higher priority to execute: the related tasks are used to solve a problem that cannot be handled by a single program

multivolume file a very large file that is stored on more than one tape reel

mutual exclusion in a multiprocessor, a method to LOCK OUT a processor from a shared resource, such as main memory: this is often accomplished through the use of a SEMAPHORE

MUX abbreviation for **MULTIPLEXER**

Mylar a trademark for a polyester made in extremely thin sheets that can be coated with a magnetic material and used in various storage devices: magnetic tape is made of Mylar

N

NAK acronym for **NEGATIVE ACKNOWLEDGE CHARACTER**

NAND 1 a logical operator connecting two propositions, each of which may be either true or false, that results in a new proposition. If both propositions are true, the new proposition is false; if at least one proposition is false, the new proposition is true **2** designating such an operation

NAND gate a gate that produces an output signal of 0 when both input signals are 1; otherwise the output signal is 1

nano– a prefix meaning one billionth

nanosecond one billionth of a second

narrowband channel in data communications, a channel with a relatively narrow bandwidth, that can transmit data at approximately 300 bits per second Compare BROADBAND CHANNEL, VOICE-GRADE CHANNEL

natural language a spoken, human language, such as English or Spanish, whose syntax and rules were developed through usage Compare ARTIFICIAL LANGUAGE

N/C abbreviation for NUMERICAL CONTROL

NDRO abbreviation for NONDESTRUCTIVE READ-OUT See NONDESTRUCTIVE READ

NE an abbreviation for NOT EQUAL TO, used as a relational operator in a program

negation a NOT operation

negative acknowledge character 1 a COMMUNICATIONS CONTROL CHARACTER transmitted by the receiving device to the sending device to indicate that the data sent has been received incorrectly: usually, the data is then automatically retransmitted **2** ACCURACY CONTROL CHARACTER

nest 1 to embed a set of instructions of one routine between the first and last instructions of another routine **2** to embed a block of data within another block of data

nested loop a loop that is nested within another loop: the first loop executes until the inner loop is encountered. The inner loop executes the specified number of times, and when it has finished, the outer loop then finishes its first execution. This process continues until the outer loop has executed the specified number of times

nested subroutine a subroutine that is called from another subroutine: the first subroutine is called from the main program and executes until it encounters an instruction that transfers control to the second subroutine. The second subroutine executes until it is finished and then transfers control back to the first subroutine

nesting level the level at which a nested routine appears within another routine

network a system consisting of a computer (or computers) and the connected terminals and related devices, such as modems and input/output channels

networking the interconnection of two or more networks

nibble a unit of storage containing half of a byte, generally four bits

nine's complement the complement of a decimal number formed by subtracting each digit from nine: for example, the nine's complement of 1234 is 8765

nine–track tape see MAGNETIC TAPE

96–column card a PUNCH CARD containing 96 columns arranged in three sections of 32 columns each: each of the 96 columns, composed of six rows for the punching of data, can represent one character. The characters corresponding to the punched holes are printed on the top of the card in three rows. The 96–column card is used on small business computers, such as IBM's System 3 Compare 80–COLUMN CARD

node **1** in a network, a hardware device or group of devices that link two or more other units to the network **2** in a data structure, such as a list or tree, an item of data, such as a record, that provides a link to other items **3** in graph theory, a junction point

noise any unwanted signal that distorts the transmission of data and results in errors in the data: noise can be caused by external sources, such as weather conditions, or by internal sources, such as the tendency of circuits and wiring to pick up pulse components from adjacent lines

nominal data data in which each value represents a distinct category, and the value itself serves merely as a label or name, with no assumption of ordering or distances between categories: for example, the classification of students by sex is nominal data, since there is no implied ordering Compare ORDINAL DATA

nonaddressable designating a storage location that cannot be accessed through an instruction: for example, in order to protect the system from inadvertent or unauthorized alteration, certain locations in memory assigned to the operating system are nonaddressable

nonconjunction a NAND operation

nondestructive read a READ that does not alter the contents of a storage location: also called a **nondestructive readout** Compare DESTRUCTIVE READ

nondestructive storage ROM

nonerasable storage ROM

nonexecutable statement a programming statement in a high–level language, that provides information about data or the way in which processing is to be done but does not cause any operations to be performed Compare EXECUTABLE STATEMENT

nonimpact printer a printer that forms DOT-MATRIX CHARACTERS or FULLY FORMED CHARACTERS, one at a time, by means of electronic, chemical, or heat signals that are transferred to paper See ELECTROSTATIC PRINTER, INK-JET PRINTER, LASER PRINTER, THERMAL PRINTER

nonlinear function a FUNCTION that is not linear and does not graph to a straight line, such as $y = a + bx + cx^2$, where a, b, and c are real numbers and x and y are variables: a specific example would be $y = 2.0 + 3.5x + 1.5x^2$. The graph of a nonlinear function is a continuous curve

non-return to zero a recording method in which a binary 1 is represented by a change in magnetization, and a 0 is represented by the absence of change, without restoring the magnetization to the neutral (zero) condition between bits Compare RETURN TO ZERO

non-switched line LEASED LINE

nonvolatile designating memory that retains data when the power supply is disconnected Compare VOLATILE

no-op clipped form of NO-OPERATION an instruction that does not specify an operation to be performed, but advances execution to the next instruction in sequence

NOR 1 a LOGICAL OPERATOR connecting two propositions, each of which may be either true or false, that results in a new proposition. If both propositions are false, the new proposition is true; if one or both propositions are true, the new proposition is false: for example, in the statement, "IF A=1 NOR B=1 THEN C=1," A=1 and B=1 must both be false for C to equal one; otherwise C is equal to zero **2** designating such an operation

NOR gate a gate that produces an output signal of binary 1 when both input signals are 0; otherwise the output signal is 0

normal form the representation of a FLOATING-POINT NUMBER in which the most significant digit in the fractional part is anything but a zero

normalized number a FLOATING-POINT NUMBER that has been converted to normal form: most computers automatically create normalized numbers as a result of floating-point operations in order to retain the maximum number of significant bits

NOT 1 a LOGICAL OPERATOR having the property that if a proposition is true, the NOT of that proposition is false, and vice versa **2** designating such an operation

NOT-AND NAND

NOT-AND gate NAND GATE

NOT gate INVERTER

NOT-OR NOR

NOT-OR gate NOR GATE

NRZ abbreviation for NON-RETURN TO ZERO

ns abbreviation for NANOSECOND

nucleus those routines in the OPERATING SYSTEM responsible for handling the basic system functions, such as input/output operations and the scheduling of jobs to be executed, that are kept in main memory while the computer is operating

NUL clipped form of NULL CHARACTER

null **1** emptiness, or the absence of information, as distinguished from zero or blank, denoting the presence of no information **2** amounting to zero

null character **1** a character, used to fill space in a storage device, that may be inserted in or removed from a sequence of characters without affecting the meaning of the sequence **2** a COMMUNICATIONS CONTROL CHARACTER used to fill time in synchronous transmission

null cycle the time it takes to execute a program without including data: it represents the minimum CPU time used by a program

null string a string that does not contain characters, as before it has been initialized

number base BASE NUMBER

number cruncher a computer designed to perform large numbers of scientific calculations: the ALU in a number cruncher can perform arithmetic operations at a rate as high as 12 million per second

numeric clipped form of NUMERICAL pertaining to data represented by the digits 0 through 9, often with such symbols as − (for negative), + (for positive), and . (for the decimal point). The numbers 4.2, + 6, −5.25 are examples of numeric data

numerical control automatic control of a process performed by a device that operates by means of instructions introduced in the form of numbers: numerical control may be used in production systems, as to control drilling or boring machines

numeric character DIGIT

numeric pad a set of numeric keys on some terminals, adding machines, or keypunches, that are grouped together in a rectangular block so that numeric data can be entered more efficiently

O

object code machine code that is the output produced by a COMPILER or an ASSEMBLER

object machine the computer on which a particular object program is executed or to be executed

object module the machine language program, or a portion of such a program, that is output from an assembler or compiler and is then processed by a LINKAGE EDITOR before it is executed

object program the program in machine language that is the output from a COMPILER or an ASSEMBLER: the object program may be in executable form or may require further processing by a LINKAGE EDITOR or LINKING LOADER

OCR abbreviation for OPTICAL CHARACTER RECOGNITION the process of reading characters that have been typed or printed in a special standardized type font: the data is read by an optical scanner as it passes under a photoelectric device and is recorded on a magnetic tape or disk. OCR is commonly used to read the information imprinted upon a receipt when a credit card purchase is made

octal designating a situation in which there is a choice of eight different possible values or states

octal number system the base 8 number system that represents an octal number as the sum of successive powers of 8: for example, the octal number 4237 can be expressed as $(4 \times 8^3) + (2$

$\times 8^2) + (3 \times 8^1) + (7 \times 8^0)$, where $8^0 = 1$, and is equivalent to the decimal number 2,207

odd–even check PARITY CHECK

odd parity see PARITY BIT

OEM abbreviation for ORIGINAL EQUIPMENT MANUFACTURER

off–line designating or of a system or equipment not directly connected to the computer and, therefore, not under the control of the CPU, such as a KEYPUNCH Compare ON–LINE

off–line operation an operation performed by off–line equipment: off–line operations are usually performed to prepare data to be entered into a computer: for example, an off–line scanner reads data from a form and copies it onto a tape that can then be read by the computer

one–address computer a computer in which each machine instruction contains one address, either that of an operand or of the storage location for the result: any other operand is assumed to be in a storage location called an ACCUMULATOR Compare FOUR–ADDRESS COMPUTER, THREE–ADDRESS COMPUTER, TWO–ADDRESS COMPUTER

one–pass assembler an assembler that scans a source program once to produce the OBJECT PROGRAM and ASSEMBLY LISTING Compare TWO–PASS ASSEMBLER, THREE–PASS ASSEMBLER

one's complement the COMPLEMENT of a binary number formed by changing all the ones to zeros and all the zeros to ones: the one's complement can be used in the computer for representing a number that is to be subtracted from another number Compare TWO'S COMPLEMENT

one–way only operation a SIMPLEX mode of operation for a DATA LINK Compare TWO–WAY ALTER-

NATE OPERATION, TWO-WAY SIMULTANEOUS OPERATION

on-line designating or of a system or equipment that is under the control of the CPU, such as terminals, disk drives, and printers: on-line systems and equipment cannot operate when the CPU is not operating Compare OFF-LINE

on-line operation an operation that is performed under the control of the CPU; more specifically, an operation in which data entered from a terminal is immediately processed by the CPU to alter the contents of a record stored on disk

OP code (AHP code) clipped form of OPERATION CODE the part of a machine or assembly language instruction that specifies the operation to be performed, such as an add, subtract, or store operation: the other part of the instruction specifies the OPERAND

open in a program, to make a file available for reading or writing Compare CLOSE

open loop in PROCESS CONTROL, the type of system in which a computer will print a message in response to feedback from a sensor or control equipment, which then requires the intervention of a human operator: for example, the message could indicate that an electrical current should be turned off Compare CLOSED LOOP

open shop the operating policy of a computer center in which any programmer or user of the computer is permitted to operate the equipment without professional assistance: most minicomputer installations operate as open shops due to the relatively low cost of the equipment and the ease with which it is operated Compare CLOSED SHOP

open subroutine a subroutine that is written at each location where it is required in the main program: it contains only the instructions needed to perform the calculations and is used when the number of its instructions is so few that integrating them into the main program requires less storage than would be needed to call a CLOSED SUBROUTINE. This implementation of a subroutine is referred to as **in–line coding**

operand 1 the part of the machine or assembly language instruction that contains the address (or addresses) of data for storage or retrieval 2 the data upon which an operation is performed: for example, in the expression $1 + 2$, 1 and 2 are operands

operating ratio AVAILABILITY

operating system a collection of system programs that controls the overall operation of a computer system: it is normally composed of three basic types of program, called the JOB CONTROL PROGRAM, the INPUT/OUTPUT CONTROL SYSTEM, and the PROCESSING PROGRAM. An operation can rarely, if ever, be performed in a computer without the assistance of an operating system

operating system monitor SUPERVISOR

operation an action or actions performed by a computer in response to an instruction

operation code OP CODE

operations research in mathematics, the quantitative study of operations in action, such as a production line or inventory system: details about the operation are observed and analyzed, theories are formulated to simulate behavior, and results are used to predict changes in resources, such as manpower, equipment, etc.

See MATHEMATICAL PROGRAMMING, LINEAR PROGRAMMING

operator see COMPUTER OPERATOR, ARITHMETIC OPERATOR, LOGICAL OPERATOR, RELATIONAL OPERATOR, CONCATENATION OPERATOR

operator console a unit used by a computer operator to monitor activity in the system, to enter information into the computer, such as the current date and time, or to begin executing a specific program: the number of components in the console varies with the type and size of the computer: for example, a large system may have a CONTROL PANEL and several display terminals and printers

optical character recognition OCR

optical mark reader a reader that senses the presence of graphite pencil marks in predetermined positions in grids on a form and records the data on magnetic tape, disk, or punched cards: optical mark readers are commonly used to read the answers on computer–graded test papers

optical scanner see OCR

optimize to obtain the best solution to a problem, as by arranging the data and instructions in such a way as to use a minimal amount of computer time in executing the program

OR **1** a LOGICAL OPERATOR connecting two propositions, each of which may be either true or false, that results in a new proposition. If one or both propositions are true, the new proposition is true; if both propositions are false, the new proposition is false: for example, in the statement, "IF A=1 OR B=1 THEN C=1," A or B must equal one for C to equal one; otherwise C is equal to zero **2** designating such an operation

order 1 a defined sequence of items according to some rule: for example, items can be in ascending, descending, or alphabetical order 2 to so sequence items of data 3 a command or instruction

ordinal data data that can be ranked according to some criterion, with each category having a unique position relative to other categories: for example, the classification of college students as freshmen, sophomores, juniors, and seniors is ordinal data Compare NOMINAL DATA

OR gate a gate that produces an output signal of binary 0 when both input signals are equal to 0; otherwise the output signal is 1

origin the absolute address of the beginning storage location in main memory for a program, used as a reference point for relative addresses

original equipment manufacturer a vendor who purchases a computer from a manufacturer, supplies it with additional hardware and/or software developed for specific applications, and sells it as a package

OS abbreviation for OPERATING SYSTEM

oscilloscope an instrument, used in hardware testing and debugging, that displays by means of a wave on a CRT the characteristics of signals, such as their size, duration, quality, and shape

out–of–line coding see CLOSED SUBROUTINE

output 1 designating any of the devices involved in printing or storing the results of computer processing 2 designating the data that results from computer processing 3 to so print or store data 4 such devices or data Compare INPUT

output–bound designating a device that is limited by the rate at which data can be output from another device, as a computer attached to a slower printer Compare INPUT-BOUND

output device a device that can provide for only the output of data, such as a printer or card punch

output job queue a queue used to store programs that have executed and are waiting to print Compare JOB QUEUE

output job stream OUTPUT STREAM

output stream the output, JCL messages, and diagnostic messages resulting from a JOB STREAM

output work queue OUTPUT JOB QUEUE

overflow 1 a condition occurring when the result of an arithmetic operation is too large to be stored in the available register: for example, an 8-bit register is capable of storing a binary number in the range of -128 to $+127$. If an addition produces a binary number larger than this range, overflow will result Compare UNDERFLOW **2** a condition occurring when a record cannot be stored on the designated track because the track is full

overflow check a test performed by the computer to determine if overflow has occurred

overflow indicator a CHECK INDICATOR used to signal that overflow has occurred

overhead SYSTEM OVERHEAD

overlap to perform two or more operations at the same time: for example, computations can be overlapped with the transfer of data between main memory and input/output devices

overlay 1 a section of a program that is temporarily stored on a DIRECT ACCESS STORAGE DEVICE while another section of the same program is executing: it is then loaded into main memory in the same locations occupied by the last section of the program that executed. Overlays are used when the program requires more memory space than is available in main memory 2 to so load a section of a program

overlay segment a segment of a program that is stored in the same storage locations in main memory as those used by other segments of the same program

overrun error an error that occurs when a transmitted character arrives before the previous character has been read: an error signal is generated to indicate the loss of the previous character so that it may be retransmitted

overstrike to print a character in the same position where that character or another one has already been printed, often as a way of highlighting the character

P

PABX abbreviation for PRIVATE AUTOMATIC BRANCH EXCHANGE a term currently used interchangeably with PBX: originally, a customer–owned private telephone system

pack to combine two or more items into one word to reduce storage space, as in a PACKED DECIMAL or in one number that represents two or more items: for example, one could use the number 111485 in one field to represent an identification number of 111 and a department number of 485 Compare UNPACK

packaged program SOFTWARE PACKAGE

packed decimal a decimal number stored in a single word in a such a way that each byte contains two digits, rather than one, in order to save storage space: the byte farthest to the right contains the sign

packet a group of bits, including data and control information, such as a source and destination address, an identification number, and error control information, transmitted as a unit

packet switching in data communications, a technique in which data is sent from a sending to a receiving terminal or computer in packets of fixed length (usually 1000 bits): each packet is sent separately and may be interspersed with packets from another location Compare CIRCUIT SWITCHING, MESSAGE SWITCHING

packing density DENSITY

pad FILL

page a portion of a program, typically 4096 bytes See PAGING

paged memory management PAGING

page fault an interrupt that occurs when a program needs an item of data or an instruction that is not currently in main memory: this allows the software to transfer the page containing the required data or instruction to main memory from external storage See DEMAND PAGING

page frame an area of main memory capable of storing one PAGE See PAGING

page printer a printer that determines the characters for an entire page within itself before printing it on paper See LASER PRINTER Compare LINE PRINTER, CHARACTER PRINTER

paging a technique for the allocation of main memory space, in which memory is divided into fixed-size blocks (called **page frames**), and programs and data are divided into blocks of that same size (called **pages**): the operating system assigns page frames only to those pages of a program that are active. The other pages are stored on a DIRECT ACCESS STORAGE DEVICE and can be swapped into main memory as they are needed

paging rate the average rate at which pages are being transferred between main memory and a DIRECT ACCESS STORAGE DEVICE at a given point in time

PA key abbreviation for PROGRAM ATTENTION KEY

paper tape a continuous strip of paper about one inch wide with five to eight parallel tracks that run along the length of the strip: characters are represented in binary format by patterns of holes punched across the width of the strip. Paper tape can be used as an input or output storage medium

paper–tape punch an automatic device that translates and records data from the main memory of a computer onto PAPER TAPE

paper–tape reader a device that reads data from a punched paper tape: as the tape moves through the reader, the presence or absence of holes is sensed and converted into electrical pulses that can be interpreted by a computer

parallel computer a computer in which addition is performed by simultaneously adding all the bits in one binary number to those in another and then adding the resulting carries to form the sum Compare SERIAL COMPUTER

parallel printer LINE PRINTER

parallel processing the simultaneous perform- ance of two or more tasks in a computer: for ex- ample, an instruction can be executing while another instruction is being read from main memory

parallel–search storage ASSOCIATIVE MEMORY

parallel transmission the transmission of the bits representing a character simultaneously over several lines: parallel transmission is faster than serial transmission but requires more lines between sending and receiving locations Compare SERIAL TRANSMISSION

parameter a variable or a constant that is transferred to and from a subroutine and a main program

parentheses–free notation the prefix or postfix notation for a mathematical expression in which the need for parentheses is eliminated since each operator, such as + or –, may only have a fixed number of operands: addition, multiplication, and division have two operands and the negation operator has one, so that subtraction is performed by the addition of a negative number: for example, the expression A + (–B) can be written without parentheses in prefix notation as +A–B, and in postfix notation as AB–+ See POSTFIX NOTATION, PREFIX NOTATION

parity bit a CHECK BIT appended to a unit of data to make the sum of the total bits even or odd: a unit of data, such as a byte or word, is considered to have even parity if the sum of the bits, including the parity bit, is even. It is considered to have odd parity if the sum is odd. A computer system is designed to assign only one type of parity throughout the system

parity check a CHECK performed by testing a unit of data, such as a byte or word, for either odd or even parity to determine whether an error has occurred in the reading, writing, or transmission of data: for example, when a unit of data is read, the parity bit is calculated and compared to the parity bit already appended to the data. If they are equal, the data is assumed to be correct; otherwise, a parity error has been detected and the data is read again

parity error an error that occurs when a unit of data, such as a byte or word, is found to have parity that is inconsistent with the system: for example, in a system testing for even parity, a unit of data found to have odd parity causes a parity error See PARITY BIT, PARITY CHECK

parsing the process of separating a programming statement into the basic units that can be translated into machine instructions: this process is performed by a language processor according to the defined rules in a given programming language

partition 1 an area of fixed size in main memory: in a multiprogramming environment, main memory can be divided into partitions, each containing a varying number of bytes. Each program specifies the partition it will use and waits its turn for that partition to become available. A computer operator can alter the sizes of the partitions **2** to so divide main memory

partitioned data set a number of logically related, sequential files, each of which is called a member, that are stored together and identified by one data set name: an index is stored with the data set containing the name of each member and its location

PASCAL a programming language, named for Blaise Pascal (a French mathematician, 1623–1662), designed to support the concepts of structured programming, with each program following a precise form: it is easy to learn and is frequently used as the first programming language taught in schools

pass one complete cycle in the execution of a program or file, including reading, processing, and writing

passing parameters the process of transferring parameters between a main program and a subroutine

password a group of characters by which a user is uniquely identified when logging on to a terminal or when submitting a program for execution

patch **1** a number of instructions in machine language added to an existing object program in order to correct an error or to perform an additional task: patches are used to avoid the cost and inconvenience of recompiling a large source program. Patching in a program must be carefully documented so that future alterations are made with the new instructions taken into consideration **2** to so add a number of instructions

pattern recognition the recognition by a computer or other automatic device of shapes or forms or of patterns of bits or signals, in order to classify, identify, or group items

pause instruction HALT INSTRUCTION

PBX abbreviation for PRIVATE BRANCH EXCHANGE a service offered by the telephone company allowing data communications within a company by means of extension phone lines and outside the company by means of dial–up lines

PC, P PROGRAM COUNTER

PCM **1** abbreviation for PULSE–CODE MODULATION in telecommunications, a modulation technique in which the signal to be transmitted is sampled at regular intervals to determine its magnitude: this magnitude is converted to a digital pulse for transmission **2** abbreviation for PUNCH CARD MACHINE

peripheral controller I/O CONTROLLER

peripheral control unit CONTROLLER

peripheral device any device used for input/ output operations with the CPU: peripheral devices include the tape drives, disks, terminals, card readers, printers, etc., that are part of a computer system and operate under the control of the CPU

peripheral driver INPUT/OUTPUT CONTROL SYSTEM

peripheral processor INPUT/OUTPUT CHANNEL

permanent error an error that cannot be corrected, such as a DATA CHECK, and that usually causes the termination of execution of the program Compare TEMPORARY ERROR

permanent storage **1** NONVOLATILE storage **2** ROM

personal computer a relatively low–cost, portable microcomputer, generally sold with software packages and useful in word processing, maintaining a budget, storing mailing lists, playing computer games, and the like

personality module a device for adapting a PROM PROGRAMMER to the unique programming voltages, currents, and pin configurations of a specific type of PROM

PERT acronym for **P**ROJECT **E**VALUATION AND **RE**VIEW **T**ECHNIQUE a variation in the CPM technique for the management of projects in which each independent task is assigned a best, worst, and most probable completion time estimate: these are used in determining the average completion time for each task and, subsequently, in determining the critical path and overall standard deviation of completion times for the entire project See CPM

PF key abbreviation for PROGRAM FUNCTION KEY

phase modulation a MODULATION technique in which the phase of a signal is altered to differentiate between a binary 1 and 0

physical record BLOCK (sense 1)

physical unit an input/output device identified by its actual label or number Compare LOGICAL UNIT

picosecond one trillionth of a second or one thousandth of a NANOSECOND

pin any of the leads on a device, such as a chip, that plug into a socket and connect it to a system: each pin provides a function, such as input, output, control, power, or ground

ping–pong buffering DOUBLE BUFFERING

pipelining a technique for increasing the speed of a computer, in which an operation is broken into a number of independent stages that are simultaneously performed on a number of instructions, each of which is in a different stage of the operation

pixel contraction of **PICTURES ELEMENT** any of the tiny elements that form a digitized picture as on a CRT screen: each represents the degree of brightness assigned to that point in the picture

PLA abbreviation for PROGRAMMABLE LOGIC ARRAY a LOGIC ARRAY that allows the designer to determine the interconnections of gates when it is manufactured, giving complete flexibility in its functions See FPLA

platen the plate or cylinder in a printer that supports the paper on which the printing is done

platter DISK

PL/I abbreviation for PROGRAMMING LANGUAGE/I a high–level programming language that was designed to handle both scientific and mathematical problems: its advanced features and sophisticated techniques have also made it a useful language for the writing of ASSEMBLERS and COMPILERS. It has unique features not available in other current high-level languages and is especially useful in handling character strings

plotter an output device in which data is transferred from main memory or an external storage device, translated into signals, and then converted into lines or curves on hard copy, thus producing charts, graphs, engineering drawings, maps, etc. See DRUM PLOTTER, FLAT-BED PLOTTER, X-Y PLOTTER

plugboard a removable board that is manually wired to control the operation of equipment, such as a keypunch: the board is perforated to allow the wires to be inserted in various patterns

plug-compatible designating computer equipment that has been designed in such a way that it can operate with equipment and systems designed by other manufacturers

PM abbreviation for **1** PHASE MODULATION **2** PREVENTIVE MAINTENANCE

pointer an address that specifies (or points to) a storage location where data can be stored or from which it can be retrieved: any address is a pointer since it points to a specific storage location, but **pointer** most commonly refers to one stored in a record or to an index that points to another record in the file

point-of-sale terminal a terminal in a retail operation that is connected to a computer in order to collect and store data when a sale is made: the terminal has a keyboard, a display area for prices, a printer for customer receipts, a display panel that guides the operator of the terminal through the purchase, and, optionally, a wand or scanner that can read Universal Product Codes.

These terminals are used throughout large stores (or a chain of stores) to maintain inventory control

point–to–point line a communication line that connects a computer and a single terminal Compare MULTIDROP LINE

point–to–point network DISTRIBUTED NETWORK

Polish notation PREFIX NOTATION

polling 1 the process of sequentially testing each potential source of input to a computer until one is found with data ready to send, allowing it to send the data, and then continuing to test sources Compare SELECTING **2** the process of testing devices in order to determine their operational status, such as whether they are ready to transmit data or whether they are in use

popping see STACK

port a connection between the CPU and another device, such as main memory or an input/output device, by means of which data can enter or leave the computer or be transferred between the CPU and memory

portable designating a program that is easily executed on a number of different types of computer: an assembly language program is not portable because it is so closely related to a specific computer's machine language, whereas a program written in a high–level language such as COBOL or FORTRAN is portable because it is not dependent upon the machine language of the computer

portable disk pack REMOVABLE DISK

Port–a–punch card a trademark for a special type of punch card with partially perforated punch positions that can be completely removed with a pen or stylus

positional parameter a parameter that must occur in a specified position in a list of parameters

postfix notation a notation for a mathematical expression in which the operator is placed after the operands: for example, the expression AB+ is in postfix notation and represents A + B. It is also called **reverse Polish notation** because it was first developed by the Polish mathematician Jan Lukasiewicz. It is used in some programming languages and compilers since it is easily evaluated and does not require the use of parentheses and other kinds of punctuation See PARENTHESES–FREE NOTATION Compare PREFIX NOTATION, INFIX NOTATION

post–mortem the investigation of an error or malfunction

post–mortem dump a dump at the end of the execution of a program for debugging, auditing, or documentation purposes

postprocessor a program that performs various final operations on data, such as preparing it for printing or arranging it into different formats Compare PREPROCESSOR

power–down to turn the electrical power off in a computer or a component of a computer system

power–up to turn the electrical power on in a computer or a component of a computer system in order to initiate the procedure necessary to bring it UP

precision the degree to which a number is exact, based on the number of SIGNIFICANT DIGITS it contains Compare ACCURACY

prefix notation a notation for an arithmetic expression in which the operator is placed before the operands: for example, the expression +AB is in prefix notation and represents A + B. It is also called **Polish notation** because it was first developed in 1951 by the Polish mathematician Jan Lukasiewicz. It is used in some programming languages, such as APL, and in various compilers since it is easily evaluated and does not require the use of parentheses and other punctuation See PARENTHESES-FREE NOTATION Compare INFIX NOTATION, POSTFIX NOTATION

preprocessor a program that prepares data for further processing by arranging it into different formats, performing various preliminary calculations, organizing it into groups, and the like Compare POSTPROCESSOR

preventive maintenance a plan or service that is intended to prevent malfunctions in equipment through frequent cleaning, testing, and replacement of components and circuit boards Compare CORRECTIVE MAINTENANCE

primary memory MAIN MEMORY

primary track the original track on a DIRECT ACCESS STORAGE DEVICE on which data is stored Compare ALTERNATE TRACK

print bar TYPE BAR

printed circuit an electronic CIRCUIT formed by applying conductive material in fine lines or other shapes to an insulating sheet, as by printing with electrically conductive ink, by electroplating, or the like

printer an output device that converts electronic signals from the computer into human-readable form, or HARD COPY: the two major types of printers are IMPACT PRINTERS and NONIMPACT PRINTERS See also CHARACTER PRINTER, LINE PRINTER, PAGE PRINTER

printout computer output printed on paper

print position any of the various positions on a form where a character may be printed

priority an assigned level of importance given to various programs, systems, and devices that determines the order in which they will be serviced by the computer

priority interrupt a system in which an interrupt is serviced based on its priority in relation to other interrupts

private automatic branch exchange PABX

private branch exchange PBX

private line LEASED LINE

privileged instruction an instruction that is restricted to programs in the operating system in order to prevent their misuse: privileged instructions usually include those for performing input and output operations, memory protection, interrupts, and timing and control operations

privileged mode a mode of operation in which privileged instructions may be executed: if a privileged instruction is encountered when the computer is not in privileged mode, an interrupt may occur or the instruction may be ignored. The SUPERVISOR runs in privileged mode while all other programs run in SLAVE MODE

problem identification the process of determining the source of an error in a program or of a malfunction in hardware

problem–oriented language a programming language, such as RPG, designed to describe more readily the problems to be solved, rather than to specify the steps to be taken to solve the problem Compare PROCEDURE–ORIENTED LANGUAGE, MACHINE–ORIENTED LANGUAGE

problem program PROCESSING PROGRAM

problem state SLAVE MODE

problem statement a statement describing the problem to be solved by an algorithm: usually written prior to the preparation of a flowchart

procedural language PROCEDURE–ORIENTED LANGUAGE

procedure 1 a set of rules and steps to be followed in operating equipment or systems in a computer system 2 in a high–level language, a SUBPROGRAM 3 a stored set of JCL statements that set up required devices and program libraries and can be called into use by a program

procedure–oriented language a programming language, such as COBOL, designed to describe the steps necessary to solve certain types of problems Compare PROBLEM–ORIENTED LANGUAGE, MACHINE–ORIENTED LANGUAGE

process 1 to perform any of various operations in order to obtain specified results 2 a method for obtaining specified results 3 TASK

process control the use of a computer to control the continuous performance of equipment, as in industrial processes: for example, the computer could be used to control temperature, to open and close valves, or to turn electrical currents on and off See OPEN LOOP, CLOSED LOOP

processing program 1 a system program, such as a LOADER, LANGUAGE PROCESSOR, or UTILITY PROGRAM, that increases the ease with which a computer system can be used: for example, a language processor enables programmers to prepare a program in a high–level language that uses Englishlike instructions instead of preparing it in the binary code used in machine language 2 APPLICATION PROGRAM

processing unit PROCESSOR

processor **1** a device capable of performing various operations on data, such as a CPU or FRONT-END PROCESSOR **2** LANGUAGE PROCESSOR

processor-bound COMPUTE-BOUND

processor state word PSW

production program a program that is executed at specified intervals, such as a payroll program

program **1** a logically arranged set of programming statements (or instructions) defining the operations to be performed by a computer in order to achieve the desired results **2** to write a program in order to solve a problem or to control the operation of a computer Compare ROUTINE

program attention (or access) key on some keyboards, a key used to interrupt the current task so that a program can perform a function

program counter a register that contains the address of the instruction which is currently executing and that is automatically advanced to the address of the next instruction

program development tools system programs that assist in the preparation of a program and translate it into machine code for execution, such as assemblers, compilers, editors, and debug aids

program flowchart FLOWCHART

program function key on a keyboard, a key used to issue a series of commands in one stroke: such keys are usually already programmed to perform specific functions, although some systems allow users to program them to their own needs

program generator a program that writes another program, based on the specifications of the problem to be solved

program interrupt an interrupt caused by various programming errors and other occurrences, such as overflow or an attempt to divide by zero

program library a stored collection of related programs and/or routines, usually already translated into machine language

program listing a listing produced by a compiler of a source program, showing each instruction with a number next to it to indicate its sequential position in the program: any errors detected by the compiler are noted at the erroneous instruction along with a brief explanation. The listing may include a CROSS-REFERENCE TABLE and a STORAGE MAP

programmable designating a device whose operation can be controlled by a program

programmable calculator a calculator that can store and execute a program entered by the user to perform calculations that are not already built into it

programmable logic array PLA

programmable read-only memory PROM

programmable terminal a terminal containing a small computer that can execute and store programs: various programs are used to support the use of the terminal for data entry, distributed processing, local file maintenance, etc. The distinction between an INTELLIGENT TERMINAL and a programmable terminal has not been precisely defined, and therefore the terms are often used interchangeably

programmed check a check performed by software on data, as distinguished from an AUTOMATIC CHECK

programmed computer STORED-PROGRAM COMPUTER

programmed instruction COMPUTER–ASSISTED IN-STRUCTION

programmed I/O POLLING

programmed switch CONDITIONAL BRANCH

programmer a computer specialist who solves problems by writing and testing programs: a FLOWCHART may be developed by the programmer to assist in the design of the program See MAINTENANCE PROGRAMMER, PROGRAMMER ANALYST, SYSTEMS ANALYST, SYSTEMS PROGRAMMER

programmer analyst a computer specialist who defines problems by performing limited SYSTEMS ANALYSIS as well as writing the programs for their solution

programming the process of writing a program to solve a given problem, testing it to ensure its accuracy, and preparing documentation to support it

programming language the set of words, and rules governing their use, employed in constructing a program See HIGH–LEVEL LANGUAGE, LOW-LEVEL LANGUAGE, PROCEDURE–ORIENTED LANGUAGE, PROBLEM–ORIENTED LANGUAGE, MACHINE–ORIENTED LANGUAGE

programming statement a basic unit of a program, much as a sentence is a basic unit of human language, that defines an activity to be performed by the computer: each programming statement is translated by a compiler into several machine language instructions. A logical sequence of programming statements forms a program or routine

program package SOFTWARE PACKAGE

program product a copyrighted or otherwise protected program supplied by a vendor for a fee

program register PROGRAM COUNTER

program run RUN (sense 1)

program scheduler JOB SCHEDULER

program specification the detailed outline of information needed to design a program, normally including a flowchart and written description

program status word PSW

PROM acronym for **P**ROGRAMMABLE **R**EAD–**O**NLY **M**EMORY a type of ROM that can be programmed to a customer's needs: the programming is done by blowing selected fuses in order to obtain a desired bit pattern, a process called **blasting**. A PROM can be programmed only once; if an error in the programming is made or a change is needed, a new PROM must be programmed Compare EPROM, EAROM

PROM programmer a device used to produce the desired bit pattern on a PROM: each bit position contains a binary 1, or each contains a binary 0, when the PROM is purchased. The device is used to blow fuses at positions needing to be changed from 1 or 0

prompt 1 a message appearing on a display terminal that requests the operator to enter information **2** to request such data from: for example, a person logging on to a terminal may be prompted for an identification number and a password before any other activity may be performed at the terminal

proprietary program a program held under patent, trademark, or copyright by a private person or group: it may be made available for others to use on different computers subject to defined restrictions and, most commonly, for a fee

protected field an area on the screen of a CRT displaying data that cannot be erased or altered from the keyboard Compare UNPROTECTED FIELD

protected storage storage that cannot be accessed without certain specified KEYS: for example, programs are assigned various keys that allow them access to certain storage locations in main memory so that they cannot inadvertently or intentionally access locations assigned to other programs

protection key a KEY assigned to a program when it begins executing and to those storage locations in main memory it will be using, so that it cannot access other locations, with different keys, that are being used by other programs

protective ground a pin on an interface for a modem used to ground the modem according to local regulations: one of the standards used by RS–232–C and CCITT V.24

protocol a set of rules governing the communication and the transfer of data between two or more devices in a communication system: the rules define the handling of certain communication problems, such as framing, error control, sequence control, transparency, line control, and startup control. There are three basic types of protocol: character–oriented, byte–count–oriented, and bit–oriented

psec (PEE sek) acronym for PICOSECOND

pseudo code a low–level programming language, closely related to an ASSEMBLY LANGUAGE, that uses mnemonic instructions, such as STO for "store", and that must be translated into machine language before it is executed: distinguished from an assembly language in that pseudo code instructions do not have the same one–to–one correspondence with machine language instructions

pseudo–instruction an instruction in an assembly language program that gives the assembler information about how the program is to be translated: a pseudo–instruction is not translated into a machine instruction that is executed, but rather directs the assembler in the translation of the program: for example, a common pseudo-instruction, END, signals the end of the instructions that are to be translated

pseudo–OP clipped form of PSEUDO–OPERATION

pseudo–operation an operation controlling the action of an assembler

PSW abbreviation for PROGRAM STATUS (or PROCESSOR STATE) WORD a nonaddressable register containing status information about the program being executed, such as the address of the next instruction and the results from the last instruction (negative, positive, or overflow)

pulse a variation in electrical energy above or below a normal level and of given duration, such as a brief surge of voltage or current

pulse–code modulation PCM

punch **1** a device that manually or automatically makes holes in specified locations on a punch card or paper tape **2** to so make holes in a punch card or paper tape

punch card a rectangular card used to store data by the presence or absence of small holes that can be punched in specific locations on the card: the presence or absence of the holes is sensed photoelectrically by a card reader. Frequently, the top, left corner of the card is cut off to ensure the uniform placement of each card in a deck. The most common type is the

80–COLUMN CARD See also 96–COLUMN CARD, BI-NARY CARD

punch card machine UNIT RECORD DEVICE

punch paper tape PAPER TAPE

punch position any of the various locations on a punch card or paper tape where a hole may be punched

pushing see STACK

put to WRITE a record

Q

QISAM (kyoo EYE sam) acronym for QUEUED IN-DEXED SEQUENTIAL ACCESS METHOD

QSAM (KYOO sam) acronym for QUEUED SE-QUENTIAL ACCESS METHOD

query language a high–level programming lan-guage, using words closely resembling ordinary language, that provides for the easy retrieval of information from a file by entering a request on a terminal

queue a list that allows insertions at one end and deletions at the opposite end: items in a queue are usually processed on the FIFO principle, by which the first item entered is the first item to be processed: for example, the output produced by a program is generally stored on disk in a queue until a printer becomes available. As each output is printed, the next in priority is selected

queued access method any ACCESS METHOD in which the transfer of data between main memory and an input/output device is automati-cally synchronized; that is, when the last record of the block has been read, the next block to be read is already in memory

queued indexed sequential access method an extension of the BASIC INDEXED SEQUENTIAL ACCESS METHOD, in which a block of input or output data is stored in a queue in main memory, ready for use, before a READ instruction is issued: the records in the block can then be randomly accessed with the use of the index and the key for the record

queued sequential access method an extension of the BASIC SEQUENTIAL ACCESS METHOD, in which a block of input or output data is stored in a queue in main memory, ready for use, before a READ instruction is issued: the records are then sequentially accessed

queuing theory the mathematical technique concerned with probability that is applied to the solution of problems involving queues, so as to minimize delay in the jobs that are waiting to execute or print

quick–access memory SCRATCHPAD MEMORY

Qwerty keyboard the standard typewriter keyboard, with the characters "q, w, e, r, t, y" appearing on the left side of the top row of alphabetic characters, usually below the numerals

R

radix BASE NUMBER

radix point the actual or implied character (a period) that separates the integer portion of a number from the fractional portion, as in the decimal number 10.25

RAM acronym for **R**ANDOM **A**CCESS **ME**MORY a type of memory in which any location can be accessed directly without having to follow a sequence of storage locations

random access DIRECT ACCESS

random access memory RAM

random access method an ACCESS METHOD in which records are directly accessed in any order by their known address Compare SEQUENTIAL ACCESS METHOD

random file DIRECT FILE

randomizing HASHING

random number an unpredictable number composed by chance of a patternless sequence of digits: the computer can be used to produce tables of random numbers for use in mathematics and statistics, particularly for such procedures as the MONTE CARLO METHOD

random number generator a program or device that produces a specified number of random numbers: these numbers are not true random numbers since the same sequence of numbers can be generated again by using the same program

raster the pattern of horizontal scanning lines on the screen of a CRT: input data causes the beam of the tube to illuminate the correct dots on these lines to produce the required characters, curves, etc.

raw data data that has not yet been processed by a computer, although it may be in machine-readable form, such as punched cards

read 1 to sense the data stored on a device **2** the process of sensing stored data

reader a device that senses data, as on punch cards or tape, and enters it into the computer

read head an electromagnetic device used to sense data previously recorded on a magnetic storage device, such as disk or tape Compare WRITE HEAD

read–mostly memory a special type of ROM that can be programmed while it is in the computer: it is used to control the operation of the computer and is, therefore, used primarily for reading its program and is written upon only when a change is needed in the controlling program: the process of reading data from such a memory is performed much more quickly than writing data into it

read–only designating main memory storage locations or stored files that can be read but cannot be altered Compare WRITE–ONLY

read–only memory ROM

read–only storage 1 ROM **2** external storage that has been assigned a read–only privilege

readout 1 the process of reading data from main memory or an auxiliary storage device and recording the data in readable form on another device **2** the information that is so copied and recorded **3** SOFT COPY

read out to copy data from a storage device or from specific addresses in main memory onto an auxiliary storage device

read–write designating a device or operation for reading data from or writing data on a storage device

read–write head an electromagnetic device that transfers data to and from the surface of a magnetic storage device, such as disk or tape

read–write memory memory that can be read or written Compare ROM

read–write privilege the authority assigned to a program allowing it to read data from a file or write or alter data in a file Compare READ–ONLY, WRITE–ONLY

real address an absolute address in real storage Compare VIRTUAL ADDRESS

real memory REAL STORAGE

real storage main memory in a computer system using VIRTUAL STORAGE

real time the time that passes on an ordinary clock

real–time clock a clock in the computer keeping track of time: it is set to the time of day by a computer operator and can be read by programs to record the time of day on output, to calculate the amount of time spent in executing a job, and to keep track of the allocations of time to each job in a multiprogramming system

real–time processing the entering, processing by the computer, and distribution of data rapidly enough to influence decisions, physical processes, or events

real–time system a system in which inquiries and data entered on a terminal can be processed quickly enough by the computer so that decisions can be made based on the response: for example, an airline reservation system is a real–time system in which a customer can request information about flights and receive a response quickly enough to reserve a seat. The airline representative can then enter the data to indicate that one less seat is available on the flight

reasonableness check LIMIT CHECK

recall RETRIEVE

received data a pin on an interface for a modem indicating whether transmitted data has or has not been received: one of the standards used by RS–232–C and CCITT V.24

received line signal detect CARRIER DETECT

receive–only designating a device, such as a terminal, that can receive data from the computer but cannot send data to it

record 1 a group of logically related fields treated as a unit: a record contains all the information related to one subject that is needed for a given purpose, and a group of records make up a file: for example, an employee's name, address, social security number, rate of pay, hours worked, deductions, etc., would form a record in a payroll file **2** to put data onto an external storage device

record blocking BLOCKING

record count a count of the number of records in a file, often used for control purposes, such as insuring that each has been processed or that no records are missing or duplicated

record format the defined arrangement of records in a file, specifying whether they are fixed–length or variable–length and blocked or unblocked

record gap INTERRECORD GAP

recording density DENSITY

recording head WRITE HEAD

record layout the defined arrangement of fields in a record

record length the number of bytes (or characters) contained in a record

record separator a control character that identifies the boundary between two records in a file or between two that are being transmitted from one device to another

recoverable error   an error that recovery routines are able to correct or one that does not cause the termination of execution of a program, such as a rounding error

recovery   the process of resuming processing without irreparable loss of the data in the system after an error in a program or a malfunction in equipment has occurred

recovery routine   a program that attempts to correct an error that has occurred and to resume the execution of the program

recursive   designating a process in which the same operation or group of operations is repeated in order to simplify the total process to be performed: for example, the process of finding the value of 3 factorial can be recursively performed by first finding 1 factorial, then 2 factorial, then 3 factorial

recursive procedure   a procedure that repeats itself, with each repetition based in part on the results of the previous one, so as to reduce a complex problem into a series of progressively simpler problems until a solution is reached

redundancy   **1** the amount of data that can be eliminated from an item of data without losing the information to be conveyed: parity bits can be removed from data since they are used for error detection and do not add to the meaning in a message **2** DUPLEXING

redundancy check   a technique of checking for errors in data when it is read, recorded, or transmitted by using extra check bits that are not a part of the actual data, as in a PARITY CHECK or CRC

reel TAPE REEL

reentrant in a multiprogramming or timesharing system, designating a system program that can be used by more than one program at a time because it is written so that it can be interrupted at some point and can then later begin processing at the same point without loss of data to any of several programs that may be using it

reentry point the address of the instruction in a main program to which control is transferred after a subroutine has executed Compare ENTRY POINT

reference edge GUIDE EDGE

reflected binary code GRAY CODE

refresh to restore the information in or on a device as it begins to fade: for example, the characters displayed on a CRT are automatically refreshed approximately thirty times a second so that the image does not fade from the screen

regenerative memory main memory that has to be periodically refreshed in order to retain stored data

register a special–purpose storage location in the CPU that is identified by a unique name and usually has a length of one WORD: registers are used to hold data to be operated on and to provide the means for the operation to be performed See ACCUMULATOR, GENERAL REGISTER, INDEX REGISTER, SHIFT REGISTER, BASE REGISTER, ADDRESS REGISTER

relational operator any of the various operators that compare two items of data: they include $<$ for **less than**, $>$ for **greater than**, $<=$ for **less than or equal to**, $>=$ for **greater than or equal to**, $=$ for **equal to**, and $\neq$ for **not equal to**

relative address an address in a program that is a specified number of bytes from another known address: for example, the relative address "0004" indicates that the data is stored four positions from another address Compare ABSOLUTE ADDRESS, SYMBOLIC ADDRESS

relative addressing an addressing mode in which a relative address is added to another address to determine the storage location used to store or retrieve data

relative code a program or instruction in which relative addresses are used to store or retrieve data: each instruction is written as if the first instruction of the program were placed in the storage location "0000" and each subsequent instruction references storage locations by addresses expressed as a number of positions away from "0000". When relative code is brought into main memory, it is placed in a set of contiguous storage locations. The first storage location in the sequence is called the **base address** and is added to every relative address in the program to determine the storage location being referenced: for example, if the base address is "2100" and an instruction to store data has a relative address of "0150", the data will be stored at "2250"

reloadable control storage an area of main memory reserved for storing microprograms that allows a microprogram to be loaded for execution, as distinguished from a CROM, used only for permanent storage

relocatable designating a program that can be moved and executed in any group of contiguous storage locations in main memory Compare MEMORY–DEPENDENT

relocating loader a loader that adjusts the addresses in a program in order to move it to the storage locations it will be using when it executes: programs are written as if the address of the first instruction will be at zero in main memory. The relocating loader adds the actual address that has been assigned to the first instruction, to all the addresses in the program, allowing the program to execute at these new locations

relocation the process of moving all or part of a program from one group of contiguous storage locations in main memory to another: relocation allows programs to execute in any available space in main memory and is necessary in a multiprogramming system where a variety of programs execute at the same time. A program may be swapped out to allow another program to execute and then swapped back into main memory and stored in a different set of locations

relocation register BASE REGISTER (sense 2)

remote designating devices that are connected to the computer through a COMMUNICATION LINK and are physically located away from the central computer site Compare LOCAL

remote access the ability to use a terminal or terminals to send data to, and receive data from, a distant computer via communication lines

remote batch processing batch processing of jobs entered at a card reader or terminal located away from the central computer site: the entire job is transmitted to the computer by communication lines, executed, and then transmitted back to the remote site for printing, or it may be printed at the central site

remote job entry the inputting of a program by means of a card reader or terminal located at some distance from the central computer

remote terminal a terminal located away from the central computer site, usually connected to the computer by a communication line Compare LOCAL TERMINAL

removable disk a disk or disk pack that can be removed from a disk drive, enabling the drive to be used by other disks Compare FIXED DISK

repeat–action key TYPAMATIC KEY

repertoire clipped form of INSTRUCTION REPERTOIRE See INSTRUCTION SET

report generator a PROGRAM GENERATOR that writes a program to produce a report

report program generator RPG

reproducer a machine that reproduces one or all of the fields on a punch card onto a number of succeeding cards and that may also be capable of punching summary data into various fields

reproducing punch an earlier device used to duplicate mechanically the data from one PUNCH CARD onto another

reproduction the process of copying data, as from punch cards, onto others of the same medium

request for price quotation RPQ

request to send a pin on an interface for a modem, that puts the modem into a transmit mode of operation rather than a receive mode: one of the standards used by RS-232–C and CCITT V.24

reserved words names that have preassigned meanings in a programming language and may only be used for specific purposes in a program

reset to return a storage location, a register, or a device to a specified, original condition or value

resident designating a program, especially a system program, that is permanently stored in main memory or in a particular storage device

resident loader a loader that is permanently stored in main memory

resource any part of a computer system, such as the CPU, main memory, an input/output device, a file, software, or personnel, that is required by a job or task

resource allocation the assignment of a resource, such as main memory or disk, to a program by the operating system

resource management the management of the various system resources, such as the CPU, main memory, input/output devices, and system programs, by the operating system

resource sharing the use of the same hardware and/or software by two or more computers, peripheral devices, or users

response time the amount of time that elapses between the entry of a command on a terminal and the actual response by the computer: it is affected by the number of commands being entered on terminals that use the same computer, by the complexity of the command, and the like

restart **1** the process of resuming the execution of a job at a checkpoint or at a specified step See CHECKPOINT RESTART, STEP RESTART **2** to so resume the execution of a job **3** designating such a point in a program

retrieval the process of locating a particular item of data from a file and displaying it on the terminal from which the request for such data was made

retrieve 1 to read data from main memory or from an external storage device **2** RETRIEVAL

return key 1 a key on some terminals used as an ENTER KEY **2** a key on some terminals used to return the cursor to the first position of the next line

return to zero a recording method in which each binary 1 or 0 is represented by magnetization in one of two directions, with a return to a neutral (zero) condition between bits Compare NON-RETURN TO ZERO

reverse Polish notation POSTFIX NOTATION

reverse video the display of dark characters on a light background on the screen of a CRT, as opposed to the more common display of light characters on a dark background

rewind 1 to return a magnetic tape to its LOAD POINT in order to reread it, or to its beginning to take it off the drive **2** the act of returning a tape

right justify to place data in the rightmost positions of a field so that the characters are aligned to a rightmost column position when printed Compare LEFT JUSTIFY

right shift a shift that moves each bit in a register a specified number of positions to the right

ring 1 CIRCULAR LIST **2** FILE PROTECT RING

ring indicator a pin on an interface for a modem that indicates whether the modem is receiving calling signals for data to be transmitted to it: one of the standards used by RS–232–C. In CCITT V.24 the corresponding pin is called **calling indicator**

ring network a network in which the various terminals and computers are linked together in a circular pattern, with each connected to the two nearest to it   Compare STAR NETWORK, DISTRIBUTED NETWORK, TREE NETWORK

RJE abbreviation for REMOTE JOB ENTRY

RMM abbreviation for READ–MOSTLY MEMORY

robot a machine capable of doing tasks normally performed by humans, by reacting to input signals or changes in the environment, making the necessary calculations, and then taking the required action: most existing robots are used in industrial settings

robotics the field of ARTIFICIAL INTELLIGENCE that deals with the design, production, and use of robots

rollback CHECKPOINT RESTART

roll in SWAP IN

roll out SWAP OUT

ROM acronym for **R**EAD–**O**NLY **M**EMORY a type of memory chip that can be read but cannot be written on or altered: ROM provides permanent storage for program instructions and is most often used in microprocessors that always execute the same program, such as a BOOTSTRAP LOADER or a program for an electronic game. A ROM is prepared by the manufacturer and cannot be altered once the chip is made. Other types of memory that can only be read are also referred to as ROMs, since they are used for the same purpose, even though they may be altered through special techniques See PROM, EPROM, EAROM

root segment the portion of a program that remains in main memory and is responsible for calling other portions to overlay one another during its execution

ROS abbreviation for READ–ONLY STORAGE

rotational delay the amount of time it takes for the recording surface of a DIRECT ACCESS STORAGE DEVICE to rotate to the proper position under the read–write head: rotational delay can be used in estimating ACCESS TIME and is expressed in milliseconds

round (or round off) to delete one or more LEAST SIGNIFICANT DIGITS of a number and deal with the remaining digits according to a predetermined rule See ROUND DOWN, ROUND UP

round down to round without making any adjustment to the remaining LEAST SIGNIFICANT DIGIT, if the leftmost of the deleted digits is equal to less than half of it: for example, 24.9743 can be rounded down to 24.97 Compare ROUND UP

rounding error the error that results from rounding off a number: for example, if the number 5.7634 is rounded off to 5.76, the rounding error is .0034

round–off error ROUNDING ERROR

round robin in a multiprogramming system, the process of executing programs one after another, in a sequence: each program is allocated a specific period of time

round up to round by adding one to the remaining LEAST SIGNIFICANT DIGIT, if the leftmost of the deleted digits is equal to half or more than half of it: for example, 98.3479 can be rounded up to 98.35 Compare ROUND DOWN

routine a set of instructions to solve a specified problem, such as those to find the square root of a number

routing INFORMATION ROUTING

row–binary designating the representation of a binary number in each row of a punch card: for example, an 80–bit binary number could be represented in one row of an 80–COLUMN CARD Compare COLUMN–BINARY

RPG abbreviation for REPORT PROGRAM GENERATOR a high–level programming language in which the specifications for a program, such as the files and the description of the records to be used, the arithmetic and/or logic operations to be performed, and the format of the printed report, are entered by the programmer: the computer generates a program that prepares the report to be printed. RPG is commonly used in businesses for simple, especially one–time, reports that do not require complex programs and are needed quickly

RPQ abbreviation for REQUEST FOR PRICE QUOTATION a customer request for a cost estimate for programming support and/or alterations or additions to a computer system

RS–232–C in data communications, a set of standards specifying various electrical and mechanical characteristics for interfaces between computers, terminals, and modems, including an interface consisting of 25 pins or leads, each of which is lettered and provides a function, such as timing, control, or the sending of data: adopted by the Electronics Industries Association (EIA), this set of standards is widely followed by hardware manufacturers

RTC abbreviation for REAL–TIME CLOCK

RTS abbreviation for REQUEST TO SEND

run **1** one execution of a program **2** to submit a program to the computer for execution

run book a list of the materials needed for a specific computer run, including a statement of the problem, controls, operating instructions, and the like

run time the time during which a program is executing

R/W abbreviation for READ–WRITE

RWM abbreviation for READ–WRITE MEMORY

RZ abbreviation for RETURN TO ZERO

S

SAS acronym for **S**TATISTICAL **A**NALYSIS **S**YSTEM an integrated system of programs written in PL/I, combined in one package program and designed for extensive data analysis, including data modification and programming, report writing, statistical analysis, and file handling

satellite processor a small computer that performs some of the slower, simpler operations for another, larger computer to which it is connected

scalar a quantity having magnitude but no direction in space, such as a temperature Compare VECTOR

scan 1 to examine sequentially all the records in a file in order to find those whose keys meet a specified criterion **2** such an examination

scanned interrupt an interrupt system in which each peripheral device is polled in a predetermined order so that the one with the highest priority is serviced first

scheduler JOB SCHEDULER

scheduling algorithm in a multiprogramming system, an algorithm that schedules the work to be accomplished, as in selecting the job to begin execution, the input/output operation to be started, or the output to be transferred to a printer

schema a description of the logical structure of a data base

scientific data processing that field of electronic data processing which is used for scientific research involving complex computations on relatively small amounts of data Compare ADMINISTRATIVE DATA PROCESSING

scratch 1 to erase data on a storage device **2** to delete the name of a file from a directory, such as a VTOC or CATALOG, so that the storage area occupied by the file may be used for another purpose

scratch file a temporary file used as a WORK SPACE during the execution of a program

scratchpad memory a group of general–purpose registers or storage locations used to store instructions, operands, or the intermediate results in a sequence of arithmetic or logical operations: scratchpad memory can be accessed at higher rates of speed than main memory

screen the viewing surface of a VIDEO DISPLAY UNIT

screen generator a program that is used to lay out and define the areas on the screen of a CRT that will be used for data entry and retrieval

scroll to advance (or go back) a specified number of lines in a file that is being displayed on a CRT

SDLC abbreviation for SYNCHRONOUS DATA–LINK CONTROL an IBM, bit–oriented protocol designed for master–slave systems

search 1 to scan a set of data items in order to locate those having a given property: for example, a group of records may be scanned in order to locate the ones containing a unique KEY **2** a technique for locating a particular record or data item See BINARY SEARCH, SEQUENTIAL SEARCH

secondary memory AUXILIARY STORAGE

secondary storage AUXILIARY STORAGE

second generation computer a computer of the generation classified as beginning in the late 1950s and early 1960s, characterized by physically smaller units that produced less heat and required less power because they used solid–state transistor circuitry, and that used disks as well as tape for auxiliary storage See COMPUTER GENERATIONS

sector a portion of the track on a DIRECT ACCESS STORAGE DEVICE, that is numbered and can hold a specified number of characters See DISK SECTOR

security the protection of data from unauthorized use or intentional destruction: security measures are typically built into the operating system of a computer and include the checking of passwords, identification numbers, and reading and writing privileges associated with each file

seek 1 to position the read–write head over a specified track on a DIRECT ACCESS STORAGE DEVICE, such as a disk 2 the process of so positioning a read–write head

seek delay SEEK TIME

seek time the amount of time it takes to position a read–write head over the specified CYLINDER on a DIRECT ACCESS STORAGE DEVICE: seek time is used in estimating ACCESS TIME and is expressed in milliseconds

segment 1 to divide a program that is too large to fit in the available space in main memory into portions that can be stored on an external storage device and called into main memory as they are needed for execution 2 one such portion of a program **3** one portion of virtual storage, containing a specified number of PAGES

segmentation a technique for dividing a program into segments so that only certain ones need be in main memory at any given time: this is done in order to allow for multiprogramming or to allow execution of a program that is too large for the available space in main memory

selecting the process of testing to determine whether or not a device is ready to receive data Compare POLLING

selector channel a channel between main memory and a number of input/output devices that allows only one input/output device to operate at a time: high–speed input/output devices, such as tape drives or disks, are usually connected to selector channels Compare MULTI-PLEXER CHANNEL

semantics the relationships between the words and symbols in a programming language and the meanings assigned to them

semaphore a flag variable indicating whether a shared resource can be accessed: a **critical program section** is a sequence of instructions in a program that, once started, must complete execution before another processor can access the same resource. A processor executing a critical program section will set the semaphore to 1, meaning that no other processor may access main memory. Once the section has been executed, the processor will set the semaphore to a value of 0, indicating that main memory is available

semiconductor a substance, such as germanium or silicon, whose conductivity is poor at low temperatures, but is improved by minute additions of certain substances or by the application of heat, light, or voltage: used in transistors, rectifiers, etc.

semiconductor memory a type of main memory on a semiconductor: such devices are classified as **metal oxide silicon** (MOS), in which bits are stored as on or off states, or as **bipolar**, in which the elements are magnetized in either of two directions. Semiconductor memory is VOLATILE and has a NONDESTRUCTIVE READ property Compare CORE MEMORY, BUBBLE MEMORY, THIN–FILM MEMORY

send–only designating a device, such as a terminal, that can send data to the computer but cannot receive data from it

sentinel 1 a character marking the beginning or end of a word, field, record, block, or file **2** FLAG

sequence checking the process of determining whether the records in a file are in the required order

sequence control the communication process that numbers MESSAGES to eliminate duplication, avoid loss of messages, and identify retransmitted messages: sequence control is handled by the particular PROTOCOL of the communication system

sequential access the type of access provided to data on a storage device in a serial order determined by the physical location of the data in the file Compare DIRECT ACCESS

sequential access method an ACCESS METHOD in which each record is accessed in the order in which it appears on the file, until the entire file has been accessed or until the desired record has been located Compare DIRECT ACCESS METHOD

sequential circuit an arrangement of interconnected gates and flip–flops whose output depends on the previous sequence of inputs, allowing it to store bits for a specified time: used in registers, counters, and other such devices that require the capability of storing bits Compare COMBINATIONAL CIRCUIT

sequential computer SERIAL COMPUTER

sequential file a file in which records are arranged in a specific sequence, usually based on a unique KEY in each record, and in which records must be accessed in sequence

sequential search a search method in which each record key of an ordered file is compared to the desired key until a match is found: the records are compared in the order in which they appear in the file. This is the simplest, although slowest, type of search Compare BINARY SEARCH

sequential storage device a storage device, such as a magnetic tape, that provides sequential access to the data stored on it and that has an ACCESS TIME dependent upon the location of the data, since an item can be accessed only by first reading through the preceding data

serial access SEQUENTIAL ACCESS

serial computer a computer in which an addition is performed by adding bits in a binary number one at a time to those in another until a sum is formed: if a carry results from the addition of a pair of bits, it is added to the sum formed by the next two bits Compare PARALLEL COMPUTER

serial printer CHARACTER PRINTER

serial storage SEQUENTIAL STORAGE DEVICE

serial transmission the transmission of bits one at a time over a single line Compare PARALLEL TRANSMISSION

service bureau a computer center that performs data processing for customers: the data to be processed is sent to the bureau, often via a terminal, and the finished results are sent back to the customer

setup **1** the process of getting all the necessary data and input/output devices ready in order to perform a job, as mounting tapes on tape drives or changing disk packs **2** the arrangement of such data and devices

seven–track tape see MAGNETIC TAPE

sexadecimal HEXADECIMAL

SHARE an organization of users of medium and large IBM computer systems, formed to evaluate vendor–supplied products and provide the results to the vendor, and to develop conventions and procedures that allow for the exchange of software: it has developed into an organization investigating a broad variety of data processing topics

shift **1** an operation that moves each bit in a register one or more positions to the right or left: shifts are usually used to perform multiplication or division and to PACK or UNPACK data. There are three types of shifts (ARITHMETIC SHIFT, LOGICAL SHIFT, and CIRCULAR SHIFT) **2** to so move each bit in a register

shift instruction an assembly language instruction designating that a shift is to be performed on the contents of a register

shift out to shift a bit or bits out of a register during the execution of a shift instruction

shift register a register in which shift instructions may be performed See ARITHMETIC SHIFT, LOGICAL SHIFT, CIRCULAR SHIFT, LEFT SHIFT, RIGHT SHIFT

short precision SINGLE–PRECISION

signal in data communications, the information being conveyed over a COMMUNICATION LINE by means of electrical impulses

signal element a portion of a digital signal that can be distinguished from other portions of the signal, as by its duration or position: for example, a start or stop bit

signal quality detector a pin on an interface for a modem indicating whether there is a probability that an error has occurred in data received by the modem: one of the standards used by RS–232–C. In CCITT V.24, the corresponding pin is called **data signal quality detector**

sign bit a bit that signifies whether a binary number is negative or positive: the sign bit occupies a specific position, usually the leftmost position, in the binary number and is 1 when the number is negative and 0 when it is positive

signed number a number preceded by a negative or positive sign

significant digits the set of digits in a number ranging from the leftmost digit that is not a zero to the rightmost digit assumed to be relevant: the set does not include zeros used for positioning of the RADIX POINT: for example, 1234, 0.001234, and 1.234 all have four significant digits Compare LEAST SIGNIFICANT DIGIT and MOST SIGNIFICANT DIGIT

sign off LOG OFF

sign on LOG ON

sign position the leftmost bit position in a WORD, used to indicate whether a number is negative or positive

simplex designating the transmission of data in one direction only, such as from a terminal to a computer or vice versa: simplex transmission is rarely used in data communication systems since it is necessary for the computer to respond that the transmitted data has been received Compare HALF–DUPLEX, FULL–DUPLEX

simulator 1 a program or device that mathematically simulates some process or system so that it can be studied **2** a program that allows a program written for one type of computer to be executed on another computer

simultaneous processing the simultaneous operation of two or more processors, as in a CPU executing an instruction and an INPUT/OUTPUT CHANNEL executing commands for the transfer of data between main memory and an auxiliary storage device Compare CONCURRENT OPERATION

single–precision designating the use of one word to store an item of data when the number of bits in the word is sufficient for maintaining a specified precision Compare DOUBLE–PRECISION, TRIPLE–PRECISION

single stepping 1 the process of working through a program by hand, step by step **2** a troubleshooting method in which the computer is slowed down so that the engineer or technician can directly obtain information at specified processing steps

sink DATA SINK

skeletal code instructions that have been partially prepared and must be completed with various details before executing

skip 1 to pass over one or more instructions in a sequence, without executing them, when certain conditions are met **2** to pass over one or more sequential positions on a data medium, such as columns on a punch card or lines on a page

slave a device operating under the control of another device, as in a MASTER–SLAVE SYSTEM

slave mode a mode of operation in which only those instructions that are not privileged instructions may be executed: the slave mode prevents unauthorized or accidental misuse of privileged instructions. All programs are run in the slave mode except the SUPERVISOR Compare PRIVILEGED MODE

small–business computer a computer for small–business data processing, that in general requires little training for its operation, comes with software tailored to the needs of that business, and is of relatively low cost: the description of a small–business computer varies among manufacturers

small scale integration SSI

smart terminal INTELLIGENT TERMINAL (sense 1)

SNA abbreviation for SYSTEMS NETWORK ARCHITECTURE

snapshot a list of the variables and their current values that is periodically produced during the execution of a program and that can be used for debugging purposes

SNOBOL acronym for **ST**RING–**O**RIENTED SYM**BOL**IC **L**ANGUAGE a high–level programming language used for STRING MANIPULATION, PATTERN RECOGNITION, and the like, needed in such areas as linguistics and the compiling of indexes and bibliographies: it is particularly useful in searching strings to find patterns, rearranging them, and forming new ones

soft copy output that is displayed on the screen of a video display unit Compare HARD COPY

soft error TEMPORARY ERROR

soft–sectored designating a floppy disk on which records are placed to mark the boundaries of each DISK SECTOR Compare HARD–SECTORED

software programs, languages, and/or routines that control the operations of a computer in solving a given problem: software is composed of two major types of programs, called SYSTEM PROGRAMS and APPLICATION PROGRAMS

software–compatible designating computers that can execute the same programs because they use the same machine language

software house a company that writes programs for users on a contract basis

software monitor a program that collects measurements on the internal operation of a computer in order to provide information on the causes and effects of events by relating the collected measurements to the program being executed at that time Compare HARDWARE MONITOR

software package a set of prewritten programs that can be purchased for use with a specified computer to perform various duties, such as accounting, payroll, statistical analysis, inventory control, spelling and syllabification verifiers, etc.

SOH abbreviation for START OF HEADING

solid–state designating or equipped with electronic components, such as transistors and integrated circuits, that convey current by controlling electrons in solid materials without the need for heated filaments, vacuum tubes, or moving parts

SOM abbreviation for START OF MESSAGE

son file see GENERATION DATA SET

sort 1 to arrange a group of records in an order determined by a particular logic, such as a chronological or alphabetical order, so as to increase the efficiency of locating specific records **2** a technique for arranging a group of records in an order determined by a particular logic See BLOCK SORT, EXTERNAL SORT, INTERNAL SORT, ASCENDING SORT, DESCENDING SORT

sort field a specified field in a record, used to sort the records of a file

source DATA SOURCE

source data automation the process of collecting data, as it occurs, in machine–readable form, as in the scanning of Universal Product Codes with a point–of–sale terminal

source document the form on which data is written and from which it is keyed into a terminal or onto a punch card

source language the high–level language, such as COBOL or FORTRAN, in which a program is written: it is translated into machine language for processing by the computer

source listing PROGRAM LISTING

source module SOURCE PROGRAM

source program a program written in a source language before it is processed by an assembler, compiler, or interpreter

SP abbreviation for STACK POINTER

space condition in data communications, the binary 0 condition or state of an electrical current Compare MARK CONDITION

special–purpose computer a computer designed to perform certain types of specialized operations: such a computer might be found in a scientific laboratory, where it performs complicated mathematical operations. Although usually highly efficient and much faster than a general–purpose computer, it performs only a

limited number of functions   Compare
GENERAL–PURPOSE COMPUTER

special symbol (or **character**) a character other than a letter or number, such as #, $, or &

specific address ABSOLUTE ADDRESS

specific code ABSOLUTE CODE

speech recognition the recognition of speech wave patterns by a computer that matches them with the stored speech patterns of words: currently being developed as a technique for orally entering data and inquiries to a computer

speech synthesis the production of speech sounds in a computer by means of analog circuits that respond to digital instructions for reproducing all the standard phonemes of a language, which are programmed in ROMs, employing a device containing filters, oscillators, and voltage–control amplifiers to simulate the sounds

split screen the screen of a CRT that is capable of displaying a portion of a file on one part of the screen and another portion of the same or some other file on another part

SPOOL acronym for **S**IMULTANEOUS **P**ERIPHERAL **O**PERATIONS **ON**–**L**INE a system program that handles data to or from lower–speed input/output devices, such as card readers and printers, by spooling it to higher–speed devices, such as disks, where it can be transferred to and from the computer more quickly

spooling the procedure by which programs and output can be temporarily stored until their turn to execute or print

SPSS abbreviation for STATISTICAL PACKAGE FOR THE SOCIAL SCIENCES an integrated system of programs, combined in one package program, designed for the analysis of social science data:

SPSS is written in FORTRAN and is designed to run on a large variety of operating systems and computers

SSI abbreviation for SMALL SCALE INTEGRATION the amount of integration on the earliest chips, typically fewer than 10 gates Compare MSI, LSI, VLSI

stack a list that allows insertions and deletions at one end only: items in a stack are usually processed on a LIFO principle, by which the last item entered is the first to be processed. The insertion of an item into the stack is called "pushing" because the item is inserted at the top and can be visualized as pushing the others down one position. The deletion of an item is called "popping" because the item is removed from the top and can be visualized as moving every other item up one position

stacked–job processing a technique in which a series of logically related programs to be executed in a specified order are entered into the computer as one job

stacker CARD STACKER

stack pointer a register containing an address in main memory where a STACK can be used to store data for later retrieval

staging 1 the process of moving data from one storage device to another device that has a shorter access time: staging can be done either at the time when it is needed during the execution of a program, or in anticipation of such a need 2 MIGRATION (sense 2)

stand–alone designating an operation performed by a device, program, or system independently of another

standard interface an interface designed according to standards so that different types of hardware and software can be interchanged

star network a network in which all communication between various computers and terminals takes place through a central computer Compare RING NETWORK, DISTRIBUTED NETWORK, TREE NETWORK

start bit the bit that signals the beginning of transmission of a series of data bits See ASYNCHRONOUS TRANSMISSION

start of heading a communications control character indicating the beginning of headers in a message

start of message a communications control character indicating the beginning of a message

start of text a communications control character indicating that all headers have been sent and that the next data sent contains the information to be conveyed

start–stop transmission ASYNCHRONOUS TRANSMISSION

startup control the process of initiating transmission in a communication system that has been inactive: startup control is handled by the particular PROTOCOL of the communication system

statement PROGRAMMING STATEMENT

statement number a number assigned to each programming statement in a program

state transition time CYCLE TIME

state vector in a multiprogramming system, the information about a task, such as the contents of various registers, that is preserved when it is interrupted and execution is switched to another task

static allocation the allocation of resources to a program before it begins execution: they remain assigned to the program until it finishes executing Compare DYNAMIC ALLOCATION

static file a file that has a low rate of additions and deletions of records Compare VOLATILE FILE

staticizer FLIP–FLOP

staticizing cycle INSTRUCTION CYCLE

static RAM a RAM that retains stored data as long as power is supplied Compare DYNAMIC RAM

static relocation in a multiprogramming system, the assignment of a set of storage locations in main memory to a program just before it is to execute: those locations are then used by the program for all subsequent execution Compare DYNAMIC RELOCATION

static storage STATIC RAM

static storage allocation the allocation of all those storage locations in main memory required by a program just before it is to execute: the program will then use these locations for its entire execution Compare DYNAMIC STORAGE ALLOCATION

station **1** the location where a terminal or card reader and printer have been placed **2** in a data communications system, any of the devices for sending or receiving data

status register a register containing bits that reflect variously the results from the last operation performed, such as negative, positive, overflow, and other such conditions or errors

STDM abbreviation for SYNCHRONOUS TIME-DIVISION MULTIPLEXING

step JOB STEP

step restart the process of resuming the execution of a job at a specified step when the job has not previously completed its correct execution because of an error in the program or a malfunction in equipment

stop bit the bit that signals the end of the data being transmitted See ASYNCHRONOUS TRANSMISSION

stop instruction an instruction that indicates the end of instructions in a program and terminates its execution

storage 1 the process of placing data into a device capable of retaining it for long periods, from which it can be retrieved as needed 2 the retention of data 3 STORAGE DEVICE Compare MEMORY

storage allocation the assignment of space to a program in main memory or on an external storage device See also DYNAMIC STORAGE ALLOCATION, STATIC STORAGE ALLOCATION

storage capacity CAPACITY

storage cell CELL

storage cycle MEMORY CYCLE

storage device any of various devices capable of retaining data for relatively long periods of time, such as a punch card, disk, or tape

storage fragmentation FRAGMENTATION

storage interleaving MEMORY INTERLEAVING

storage location any of a series of positions in main memory, each of which has a unique address and is capable of storing one byte or word

storage map a listing or diagram of storage locations in main memory that are used by a program and/or data, in order to determine the amount of storage used and the location of various items of data

storage register MEMORY DATA REGISTER

storage unit MAIN MEMORY or any STORAGE DEVICE

store 1 to write data in main memory or on an external storage device 2 such an operation

store and forward MESSAGE SWITCHING

stored program a program stored in main memory while it is executing

stored–program computer a computer that stores the instructions in a program in main memory while they are waiting to execute: the development of the stored–program computer was significant because it eliminated the reading of instructions from a relatively slow input medium, such as paper tape, and stored them in high–speed main memory where they could be more rapidly accessed by the CPU. Digital computers are now all stored–program computers

straight–line code instructions that are executed in sequence without repetition, as distinguished from those in a LOOP: repetition is achieved only by writing the instructions again

string 1 a sequence of characters treated as a unit in a program 2 a set of record keys in a descending or ascending order

string manipulation the process of performing various string operations

string operation an operation performed on a string, such as concatenating, copying, replacing, or rearranging it or identifying various substrings within it

structured programming a programming discipline in which each sequence of instructions performing a specified logical procedure is viewed as a separate unit with one entry and exit point, so that the program can be viewed as a series of processing steps and be more easily understood: TOP–DOWN PROGRAMMING is usually considered a part of structured programming

STX abbreviation for START OF TEXT

subprogram a program that solves a particular problem for another program, but cannot execute by itself: for example, a subprogram may be used to detect errors in data before the data is used within another program

subroutine a sequence of instructions that performs a specific task, usually used more than once in a program: it may be written to perform a task that is needed repeatedly for a specific program or it may be written to perform a task commonly needed by many programs, such as one that calculates the square root of a number See OPEN SUBROUTINE, CLOSED SUBROUTINE

subroutine call in a program, an instruction that transfers control to a subroutine

subroutine library a collection of subroutines that are stored together and may be used by a number of different programs

subroutine linkage CALLING SEQUENCE

subscript a symbol or number that identifies a particular element in an array

subset 1 a smaller group of items within a larger set 2 MODEM

substring 1 a sequence of consecutive characters that is a part of a CHARACTER STRING: for example, "BASE" is a substring of "BASEBALL" 2 designating an operation in which such a sequence is identified

subsystem a hardware and/or software system for performing a specified function within a larger system

subtask a task that is started by another, logically related task of higher priority

supercomputer an extremely fast computer that can process both SCALAR and VECTOR quantities, can perform many thousands of operations simultaneously, and is capable of performing billions of additions per second

supermini a computer designed as an extension of the architecture of a MINICOMPUTER, having generally a word length of 32 bits and main storage of one million bytes or more

supervisor a group of system programs that maintains the integrity of a system, controls input/output operations, and schedules the use of the CPU resources and main memory in a multiprogramming system: the supervisor is part of the operating system and is used to monitor the running of programs in the computer so that multiple programs can execute without interfering with one another

supervisor call an instruction that interrupts a program and calls the supervisor to perform a service, such as the input or output of data, that the program cannot or is not permitted to perform See SUPERVISOR, PRIVILEGED MODE

supervisor state PRIVILEGED MODE

supervisory instruction PRIVILEGED INSTRUCTION

supervisory routine SUPERVISOR

support programs SYSTEMS SOFTWARE

SVC abbreviation for SUPERVISOR CALL

swap in to move a program from auxiliary storage into main memory for execution See SWAPPING

swap out to move a program from main memory into auxiliary storage to await further execution See SWAPPING

swapping a process that moves programs between main memory and auxiliary storage: swapping is used in a multiprogramming system to make more effective use of main memory. The operating system will swap out a program in a WAIT STATE and swap in another program that is ready to execute

switch **1** a point in a program where a BRANCH may occur depending on whether a condition is found to be true or false **2** a device in a circuit that allows or breaks the flow of electricity in that circuit

switched line DIAL–UP LINE

switching center in data communications, a device that routes data from incoming circuits to the proper outgoing circuits

symbolic address a name substituted for an address in a program: symbolic addresses make a program easier to write and understand, since English words can be used instead of numbers to refer to an address Compare ABSOLUTE ADDRESS, RELATIVE ADDRESS

symbolic code programming code that uses mnemonic names for instructions, such as SUB for subtract, and allows symbolic names to be assigned to storage locations: symbolic code is closely related to machine code and is used in low–level programming languages, such as assembly languages

symbolic logic the study of formal logic in which propositions, quantifiers, and relationships are expressed by means of an ARTIFICIAL LANGUAGE in an attempt to avoid the vagueness and inadequacies of a NATURAL LANGUAGE

symbolic parameter **1** in assembly language, a symbol that is defined in a MACRO DEFINITION and is assigned a value when the macro definition is called **2** in job control language, an arbitrarily named symbol appearing in a cataloged or in-stream procedure, that is assigned a specific value: when the procedure is called, the value is substituted for the symbol wherever it appears. Generally, a symbolic parameter is set to an initial or DEFAULT value; however, since symbolic parameters are used to allow for easy modifications of frequently changed statements, the value can be easily altered

symbol table 1 a table produced by an assembler containing each symbol used in a program and its corresponding address in the program: the table is used by the assembler to substitute the address for each occurrence of the symbol in the object program and may also be printed in the ASSEMBLY LISTING **2** a table produced by a compiler or an interpreter, containing each variable used in a program and its corresponding attributes, such as whether it is numeric or alphabetic, its length, and its format

sync character in synchronous transmission, a character periodically transmitted to the receiving device as a check on its synchronization with the sending device

synchronous designating events occurring in regular, timed intervals that are synchronized as by pulses from the computer CLOCK

synchronous computer a computer in which timed signals are used to start and stop an operation, allowing sufficient time between signals to complete the operation: the signals are sent out by a clock built into the circuitry of the computer Compare ASYNCHRONOUS COMPUTER

synchronous data–link control SDLC

synchronous device a device that transmits signals at regular, timed intervals to the system with which it is communicating Compare ASYNCHRONOUS DEVICE

synchronous time–division multiplexing a time–division multiplexing technique in which each terminal is allotted a period of time for transmitting, whether or not it has data to transmit Compare ASYNCHRONOUS TIME–DIVISION MULTIPLEXING

synchronous transmission the transmission of data from one location to another at regular, timed intervals: one device requests data from another, waits a specified length of time, and then reads the data Compare ASYNCHRONOUS TRANSMISSION

synonym a record whose key has been converted to the same hash address as another record See HASHING

syntactical analysis the process performed by a compiler in order to ensure that the rules of the programming language have been followed correctly Compare LEXICAL ANALYSIS

syntax in programming languages, the rules governing the structure of statements used in a program: for example, the statements in some programming languages must begin in certain columns and be terminated with a specific symbol, such as a period, in order to be executed properly

syntax error an error caused by a violation of the syntax of a particular language, detected by the language processor when the program is translated into machine language: if severe enough, it may prevent the program from being executed

SYSGEN (SIS jen) acronym for **SYS**TEM **GENERA**-TION

system an aggregate of hardware, software, and personnel organized to perform a function or functions

system bus the bus that carries data between various units in a computer: it consists of the DATA BUS, ADDRESS BUS, and CONTROL BUS

system description a general outline of a system, describing its objectives and various operational procedures for its use

system flowchart see FLOWCHART

system generation the process of implementing a basic software system on a specific computer: such a system is supplied by the computer manufacturer or a software vendor. A program, called a **system generator,** processes the basic system and parameters that describe a specific installation to produce a system tailored to it. System generation is used to implement new OPERATING SYSTEMS and LANGUAGE PROCESSORS or to update the existing versions

system generator see SYSTEM GENERATION

system log a file used to store data concerning job information, unusual conditions, messages to and from the computer, and operational data: this file is usually printed for documentation and is used by operators and systems programmers

system overhead the percentage of time that a computer system functions as a supervisor rather than in the performance of an actual program

system program a program supplied by the computer vendor so that the computer can be used more easily and effectively See OPERATING SYSTEM

systems analysis the analysis of a business or entire project to see how it can best be helped or accomplished using data processing

systems analyst a computer professional who is responsible for the systems analysis and design of programs for various applications

systems console MASTER CONSOLE

systems disk a disk reserved for storage of programs and data used by the OPERATING SYSTEM and of various other system programs, such as loaders, compilers, and assemblers

systems library a collection of programs used by the OPERATING SYSTEM and the various assemblers, compilers, linkage editors, and loaders

systems network architecture a description of the functional design of a data communications system, including its hardware, software, and communication links, and how they interact

systems programmer a programmer who creates, maintains, and controls the use of an OPERATING SYSTEM in order to increase productivity in a computer system

systems software a collection of SYSTEM PROGRAMS that enable the computer system for which they were prepared to be used more efficiently by a wide variety of people

T

table a collection of data for quick reference, either stored in sequential locations in memory or printed as an array of rows and columns of data items of the same type: for example, one column may contain the keys of records, and a corresponding column may specify the location of each record on a disk

table look-up the process of obtaining from a table a value based on another value in a program, such as a key for a record

tactile keyboard a keyboard that is a flat, conductive surface upon which the keys have been imprinted, used on some calculators and microcomputers: the keys are lightly touched, rather than struck

tag **1** a field or a record that contains the key to a record and the address of where it is stored in a file: for example, a tag for a payroll file record could contain an employee number and the corresponding address of that employee's record **2** SENTINEL **3** LABEL

tag file a collection of tags stored as a file and used in a program to directly access the full records stored in another file: for example, a program could first search the tag file for the key to a record, such as an employee number, find its address, and go directly to that location in the full file instead of sequentially searching the file for that particular employee

tag sort a sort of a tag file instead of the full file, for quicker retrieval of records from the original file

talk to transfer data between two devices, as between a computer and a terminal

tape **1** MAGNETIC TAPE **2** PAPER TAPE

tape comparator COMPARATOR (sense 2)

tape deck MAGNETIC TAPE DRIVE

tape drive MAGNETIC TAPE DRIVE

tape label a label that is recorded on a magnetic tape, such as a LABEL RECORD or a VOLUME LABEL, or one that is placed on the exterior of the tape reel to identify the tape visually

tape operating system an operating system that is stored on tape, rather than in main memory or on a disk, while the computer is in operation: tape operating systems are rarely used today but were an earlier alternative for many businesses that found the cost of disks prohibitive Compare DISK OPERATING SYSTEM

tape reel a roll of magnetic tape wound on a spool

tape transport MAGNETIC TAPE DRIVE

target program OBJECT PROGRAM

tariff the rate charged to customers for use of a communication channel provided by a common carrier

task **1** a program executing in the computer **2** a basic unit of work to be performed by the computer: a program may consist of a number of tasks, such as reading the records from a file

task control block information needed to manage the concurrent execution of programs, such as the priority assigned to them, the partition they will execute in, and their status

task management the management of the execution of the various tasks and the allocation of the various resources in a computer system performed by programs in the OPERATING SYSTEM, such as the DISPATCHER

task state descriptor STATE VECTOR

TCAM (TEE kam) acronym for TELECOMMUNICATIONS ACCESS METHOD

TCB abbreviation for TASK CONTROL BLOCK

TDM abbreviation for TIME–DIVISION MULTIPLEXING

technical support the functions performed by personnel in a computer center who maintain and update the OPERATING SYSTEM and other such system programs in order to make optimal use of the computer system

telecommunications the transmission of data over communication lines to and from a distant location

telecommunications access method an ACCESS METHOD that controls the transfer of data between main memory and a terminal or terminals through the use of MACROS specified by a programmer and incorporated in a program called a **message control program**

teleprinter a chiefly British term for TELETYPEWRITER

teleprocessing data processing in which terminals and communication lines are used for sending and receiving data between distant locations and a data processing center

teleprocessing system a data processing system by which programs and data can be created, updated, retrieved, stored, and submitted for execution through the use of remote terminals connected by communication lines with a central computer center

teletext an information retrieval system in which data, such as news, stock quotations, or weather, from a distant data bank can be transmitted, superimposed on a television signal, to TV receivers in homes: the receiver is provided with a special circuit to decode the signals and display in alphanumeric and graphic form on the TV screen the data, which can be called up at will. Unlike VIDEOTEX, this system does not provide for viewer input into the computer system

Teletype a trademark for a form of teletypewriter

teletypewriter a terminal with a keyboard for input and paper for printed output, generally operating at 10 to 15 characters per second and used in telegraphic data communications: it may also include a paper tape punch and reader to produce data in machine–readable form or to transmit data stored on paper tape

Telex a trademark for a worldwide data communications dial–up service for teletypewriter and paper tape communication of data

Telpak a service offered by telephone companies providing leased voice–grade channels between two or more locations for data communications

temporary data set a data set stored in a temporary location during the execution of a program: it usually contains intermediate records while they are being processed by a program, such as a partially sorted group of records

temporary error an error that is recovered by correcting the data or by retrying the read or write operation Compare PERMANENT ERROR

temporary storage an amount of space on a DIRECT ACCESS STORAGE DEVICE, or less commonly on a magnetic tape, for holding data in intermediate stages of processing during the execution of a program

ten's complement the complement of a decimal number formed by subtracting each digit from nine and adding one to the LEAST SIGNIFICANT DIGIT: for example, the ten's complement of 1234 is 8766

tera– a prefix meaning a trillion, or 10^{12}

terminal a device used by a person to send data to and receive data from a computer system; especially, such a device with a keyboard and an attached CRT and/or printer: terminals can be located at great distances from the computer, connected by any of various communication lines

test data a small sample of data, taken from a file or artificially created, used in the test run of a program

test run an execution of a program using test data to determine if any errors were made in syntax or logic when the program was written

text that portion of a MESSAGE containing the data to be conveyed, such as the line of data typed into a terminal, that is preceded by a start–of–text character and followed by an end–of–text character

text–processing the use of a terminal connected to a computer system in order to create, alter, and produce text, such as reports, manuscripts, and the like, that often require revisions and many copies

thermal printer a NONIMPACT PRINTER that prints DOT–MATRIX CHARACTERS one at a time by means of wire ends that are heated in a particular pattern for each character and that form visible dots when the wires come into contact with a specially coated, heat–sensitive paper

thimble printer an IMPACT PRINTER that prints FULLY FORMED CHARACTERS by pressing a print element in the shape of a thimble against an inked ribbon and paper: the thimble, containing two rows of characters, rotates and tips up and down to print characters from either of the two rows, one character at a time

thin–film memory main memory made by depositing extremely thin films of a magnetizable material on an insulating base, such as glass:

magnetic spots on the film are polarized by wires for storing bits. It has a non–destructive read property

third generation computer a computer of the generation classified as beginning in the late 1960s and early 1970s, characterized by physically smaller computers using integrated circuits on chips for most of its circuitry See COMPUTER GENERATIONS

thrashing in a multiprogramming system, a situation in which the computer must spend more time in PAGING than in executing programs

threaded file CHAINED FILE

three–address computer a computer in which each machine instruction contains three addresses, the addresses of both operands and the address of where the result is to be stored: the address of the next instruction is stored in a register rather than in the instruction Compare FOUR–ADDRESS COMPUTER, TWO–ADDRESS COMPUTER, ONE–ADDRESS COMPUTER

three–pass assembler an assembler that scans a source program three times: the first scan constructs a SYMBOL TABLE, the second produces the ASSEMBLY LISTING, and the third produces the OBJECT PROGRAM Compare ONE–PASS ASSEMBLER, TWO–PASS ASSEMBLER

throughput the amount of processing performed in a given amount of time by a computer or a component of the computer system

time–division multiplexing in data communications, a multiplexing technique in which bits or bytes are selected from terminals for transmission during allotted time periods See ASYNCHRONOUS TIME–DIVISION MULTIPLEXING, SYNCHRONOUS

TIME–DIVISION MULTIPLEXING Compare FREQUENCY–DIVISION MULTIPLEXING

timesharing a system of computer operation in which the rapid alternation in execution of programs allows two or more to be entered and processed in a way that appears simultaneous

time slice a designated period of CPU processing time

time slicing a scheduling method for the sharing of main memory in which a TIME SLICE is allocated to each program: each program executes during its given time slice and is then swapped out to await its turn to execute again

Tiny BASIC a high–level programming language, designed for microcomputers, that is a subset of BASIC

TIP TOP acronym for TAPE INPUT TAPE OUTPUT designating a computer system that both reads data from and writes data on magnetic tape

toggle 1 FLIP–FLOP 2 a manually operated switch with two positions, on and off

token a set of characters, such as a VARIABLE NAME, that can be identified by a compiler

top–down programming a programming discipline in which the major steps to be accomplished are first identified, programmed, and tested: the lesser steps within each major step are then added to the program as they are written and tested

TOS acronym for TAPE OPERATING SYSTEM

total system a data processing system in which all significant operations are performed as the data occurs, and in one central location, so that the effect of altering data is immediately apparent to all relevant programs

trace **1** a program or routine that produces for debugging purposes a listing of each instruction in another program and the values resulting from each operation **2** to perform such an operation

track **1** any of the concentric paths for the recording of data on the surface of a DIRECT ACCESS STORAGE DEVICE, such as a disk or magnetic drum **2** CHANNEL (sense 1)

track ball a sphere mounted in a box so that it can be rotated with the palm of the hand or fingertips, and connected to a terminal, in order to move the cursor to any position on the screen of a CRT: commonly used in computer graphics and many types of computer games

track density the number of adjacent tracks per unit of distance on a storage device, such as magnetic tape or disk

track pitch the distance between corresponding points of adjacent tracks on a storage device, such as magnetic tape or disk

traffic the volume and flow of messages being transmitted in a computer system

trailer label a label record, stored at the end of a file on magnetic tape, that signals the end of the file and contains summary information, such as a count of the number of records in the file Compare HEADER LABEL

trailer record TRAILER LABEL

trailing edge **1** designating a decision as to whether a loop has executed the specified number of times, placed at the end of the loop so that the loop is executed before the counter is tested **2** the portion of a pulse during its transition from binary 1 to 0 Compare LEADING EDGE

train printer an IMPACT PRINTER that prints FULLY FORMED CHARACTERS one line at a time by striking

TYPE BARS suspended from a continuously rotating train of carriers against an inked ribbon and paper See LINE PRINTER

transaction any event about which data is recorded and processed, such as the deposit or withdrawal of a sum of money in or from a bank account

transaction file a group of transaction records collected on a periodic basis and stored for later use in updating a MASTER FILE

transaction record a group of fields containing information about one transaction

transceiver a terminal that can both transmit and receive data

transcribe to copy data from one storage device to another, with or without altering its format

transducer a device that converts energy from one form to another, as in card readers, printers, or terminals that transform electrical signals into human–readable form or vice versa

transfer **1** to move data from one location to another **2** such an operation **3** BRANCH

transfer rate the rate at which data is transferred between a storage device and main memory: transfer rate is expressed in bits, bytes, or characters per second

transient GLITCH

transient error INTERMITTENT ERROR

translating program TRANSLATOR

translator a program that converts a program written in one language to another language See COMPILER, ASSEMBLER, INTERPRETER

transmission DATA TRANSMISSION

transmission control character COMMUNICATIONS CONTROL CHARACTER

transmitted data a pin on an interface for a modem used to transmit data: one of the standards used by RS–232–C and CCITT V.24

transmitter (or receiver) signal element timing a pin on an interface for a modem, that provides the transmitting (or receiving) section of the modem with timing information: one of the standards used by RS–232–C and CCITT V.24

transparency in data communications, the characteristic of transmitted data containing bit patterns resembling specific control characters: this characteristic may cause the receiving device to interpret the bit pattern incorrectly. The PROTOCOL of a communication system provides the means for correcting transparency

trap **1** an interrupt caused by an exceptional condition, such as an attempt to divide by zero, overflow, or an attempt to use a privileged instruction: a trap is activated by hardware that automatically transfers control to the OPERATING SYSTEM **2** loosely, INTERRUPT

tree a data structure in which records are stored in a hierarchical manner: one node (record) is designated as the root and each subsequent node branches from the root or from another subsequent node of higher level, according to the rules defining the relation between nodes

tree network a network in which the various terminals and computers are linked to a main computer in a hierarchical manner, with each additional device branching from one of a higher level Compare STAR NETWORK, DISTRIBUTED NETWORK, RING NETWORK

trigger **1** INVERTER **2** a pulse that initiates a function in another circuit **3** to so initiate a function

triple–precision designating the use of three words to store an item of data when they are needed to maintain a high level of precision Compare DOUBLE–PRECISION, SINGLE–PRECISION

troubleshoot DEBUG

true complement COMPLEMENT

true form the representation of a number that is stored as it is written: positive numbers are stored in true form, whereas negative numbers are most commonly stored in complement form Compare COMPLEMENT FORM

truncate to lose one or more digits from a number when it is placed in a storage location that is too small to store all the digits in the number: for example, the number 5.7689 would be truncated to 5.76 when it is stored in a location capable of holding only four characters. This results in an inaccurate number and is called **truncation error**

trunk **1** a communications channel that transfers data between two SWITCHING CENTERS, generally over long distances **2** a group of lines enclosed in a single casing

truth table a table showing all the possible combinations of the variables in an arithmetic expression and their corresponding results: a truth table is often used to show the relationship between the inputs to a logic device and the corresponding output from the device: for example, an AND GATE is described by the logic function X = A + B. The truth table for this function would have every combination of the values for A and B (00, 01, 10, 11) and the resulting value of X for each combination (0, 0, 0, 1), according to the rules for an AND gate

TTY abbreviation for TELETYPEWRITER

tube VIDEO DISPLAY UNIT

tune to adjust the hardware and/or software of a computer in order to make the most efficient use of its resources for a given workload

turnaround documents computer–readable forms, such as punch cards or OCR forms, produced by the computer and usually marked with some preliminary information that is later input as data to a program after an event has occurred: for example, a punch card could be produced for every employee containing name and employee number. Other details, such as the number of hours worked, could be manually punched onto the card, which is then returned for input to a payroll program

turnaround time 1 the amount of time it takes for a programmer or customer to receive output after submitting a program for execution **2** in HALF–DUPLEX transmission, the amount of time it takes to change the direction in which data is transmitted, i.e., from the sending location to the receiving location or vice versa

turnkey designating a computer system supplied to a customer by one vendor, complete with all the hardware, software, and training of personnel

twelve–punch a punched hole in the first row, called the twelve–row, of an 80-COLUMN CARD See ZONE PUNCH

two–address computer a computer in which each machine instruction contains two addresses, the address of each operand: the result is placed in the location previously occupied by one of the operands Compare FOUR-ADDRESS COMPUTER, THREE-ADDRESS COMPUTER, ONE-ADDRESS COMPUTER

two–pass assembler an assembler that scans a source program twice: the first scan constructs a SYMBOL TABLE, and the second scan produces the OBJECT PROGRAM and ASSEMBLY LISTING Compare ONE–PASS ASSEMBLER, THREE–PASS ASSEMBLER

two's complement the complement of a binary number formed by changing the ones to zeros and the zeros to ones and adding binary one to the result: most computers perform subtraction by the addition of the two's complement to the number it is being subtracted from Compare ONE'S COMPLEMENT

two–way alternate operation a HALF–DUPLEX mode of operation for a DATA LINK Compare ONE–WAY ONLY OPERATION, TWO–WAY SIMULTA-NEOUS OPERATION

two–way simultaneous operation a FULL–DUPLEX mode of operation for a DATA LINK Compare ONE–WAY ONLY OPERATION, TWO–WAY ALTERNATE OPERATION

TWX (TWIKS) trademark acronym for **T**ELETYPE-**W**RITER E**X**CHANGE SERVICE a data communica-tions service for two–way teletypewriter or paper–tape communications between subscrib-ers to the service

typamatic key on a keyboard, a key that, when depressed, keeps repeating the character or function until it is released

type bar a bar used for printing that contains all the characters in a particular character set: dif-ferent type bars can contain different character sets and can be used interchangeably See BAR PRINTER

type–bar printer BAR PRINTER

U

UART (YOO art) acronym for **U**NIVERSAL **A**SYN-CHRONOUS **R**ECEIVER–**T**RANSMITTER a device, usually an integrated circuit, that performs the parallel–to–serial conversion of digital data that is to be transmitted and the serial–to–parallel conversion of digital data that has been transmitted: for example, a UART converts the outgoing digital data in parallel format from a microcomputer into the serial format accepted by a MODEM

unary operation MONADIC OPERATION

unary operator MONADIC OPERATOR

unattended operation the operation of a computer system that does not require the manual intervention or presence of an operator: for example, a computer system with no tape drives or attached printers may be left in unattended operation Compare ATTENDED OPERATION

unbundled designating program packages and services that are sold separately from a computer and its basic systems software: most vendors supply unbundled packages and services Compare BUNDLED

unconditional branch a branch instruction that does not test a condition before the branch occurs Compare CONDITIONAL BRANCH

undefined designating a variable or constant that has not been assigned a specified length or data type before it is used in a program

underflow a condition occurring when the result of an arithmetic operation is a fraction too small to be stored in the available register: when underflow occurs, the register is usually set to zero and a CHECK INDICATOR is set to signal that it has occurred Compare OVERFLOW (sense 1)

unidirectional bus a bus that can transfer data in only one direction, as from the CPU to main memory or vice versa   Compare BIDIRECTIONAL BUS

uninitialized designating a counter, storage location, variable, or the like that has been set to a starting value

uniprogramming system a computer system in which jobs are brought into main memory and completely executed, one at a time   Compare MULTIPROGRAMMING SYSTEM

unit record PUNCH CARD

unit record device any of the various machines that perform operations on punch cards, such as a keypunch, collator, or sorter

universal asynchronous receiver/transmitter UART

universal character set a feature on some printers allowing any one of a variety of character sets to be chosen for printing

unpack to break a packed unit of storage into its individual components Compare PACK

unprotected field an area on the screen of a CRT where data can be entered, erased, or modified from the keyboard Compare PROTECTED FIELD

unrecoverable error ABEND

up designating a computer, a component of a computer system, or a software system, that is operating correctly and so is available for use Compare DOWN

update to change the data in a file to reflect new or more current information: for example, a MASTER FILE is updated by a TRANSACTION FILE

uptime the period during which a computer, a component of a computer system, or a software system is up Compare DOWNTIME

upward compatible designating a new version of a computer or software system, such as a language processor, that produces identical results for a program executed on the previous version Compare DOWNWARD COMPATIBLE

USASCII (YOO ES ASS kee) acronym for UNITED STATES OF AMERICA STANDARD CODE FOR INFORMATION INTERCHANGE another, less common name for ASCII

user a person who uses the computer or any of the services provided by a computer center

user friendly designating a computer, terminal, program, etc. that is easily used and understood by a wide variety of people

user library a library stored in a computer system, as one for the private use of an individual or one for general use

user program an application program written by a person other than the programmers in a computer center

user–programmable terminal PROGRAMMABLE TERMINAL

utility function a function performed by a UTILITY PROGRAM, such as the copying of data from cards or disk to magnetic tape, or the sorting or merging of files

utility program a program provided by a computer center or vendor to perform a task that is required by many of the programs using the system: common utility programs are those that copy data from one storage medium to another and sort/merge progams. Other utility programs may provide text editing, initiate the execution of programs, and perform other functions not directly related to the processing of data in a program

V

validation in a program, the process of testing data to determine whether it correctly adheres to the designated criteria, such as whether it falls within the prescribed limits, whether it is in the specified order, or the like

validity check **1** a check performed on a character to verify that it is actually a valid code **2** a validation test performed on data before processing by a program

variable a label representing a value that changes during the execution of a program: for example, a social security number is a variable that changes each time the record for a new person is read

variable–instruction–length designating a CPU that has the ability to recognize different types of instructions with varying length

variable–length character encoding the use of a variable number of bits to represent characters so that the most frequently used characters would be represented with the least number of bits, thereby reducing the amount of storage space used, as distinguished from encoding schemes using the same number of bits for each character, such as ASCII or EBCDIC

variable–length records records in a file that may vary in length, usually because the file contains two or more types of records, each of which contains different types and numbers of fields Compare FIXED–LENGTH RECORDS

variable name the name assigned to a variable in a program: for example, "IDNUM" might be the name assigned to the variable representing the employee identification number in a payroll program

variable word–length computer a computer in which the number of bits contained in a word varies depending upon the data or instruction. Each word is delineated from another word by a special bit contained in each byte: this bit is called a WORD MARK and signals the beginning and ending of a word. Variable word–length computers are BYTE–ADDRESSABLE Compare FIXED WORD–LENGTH COMPUTER

VDT abbreviation for VISUAL DISPLAY TERMINAL

VDU abbreviation for VIDEO DISPLAY UNIT

vector 1 a one–dimensional arrangement of numbers; that is, a single row or a single column **2** a quantity that has both magnitude and direction in space, such as a velocity Compare SCALAR

vectored interrupt an interrupt system in which an interrupt causes a direct branch to the routine that handles it See INTERRUPT VECTOR

verb in PROCEDURE–ORIENTED LANGUAGES, a reserved word that specifies an action to be performed, such as "ADD" in COBOL

verifier a keypunch upon which one may check data for accuracy by placing the punched cards into the hopper and reentering the original data on the keyboard: the depressed keys are then compared to the holes already punched, and the keypunch will signal if they do not match

vertical redundancy check VRC

very large scale integration VLSI

videodisc a disk used for the storage of audio and visual information to be replayed on a television screen, as for use in home entertainment or for the storage of digital data in a computer system: currently being developed for mass storage, videodiscs can store approximately 10^{10} bits

video display unit any peripheral device that displays data on a screen, such as a CRT

videotex or **videotext** an interactive information retrieval system in which data is transmitted over telephone lines between a distant computer and home television screens: unlike TELETEXT, this system provides for the entering of data, by means of a keyboard, into the computer system, as in making reservations, placing orders, carrying out banking transactions, or the like

viewdata an earlier, chiefly British, name for VIDEOTEX

virgin medium a storage medium that has never been used

virtual address an address identifying the SEGMENT number, page number within the segment, and the position of the record relative to the beginning of the page, that is used to store and retrieve pages of a program in virtual storage Compare REAL ADDRESS

virtual machine the hardware and operating system software that define the way in which a user views the computer and how it appears to execute a program: for example, in a computer system with virtual storage, the computer appears to store the entire user program in main memory while it is executing, when in fact it is stored in virtual storage and only portions of the program are brought into main memory as they are needed for execution

virtual memory VIRTUAL STORAGE

virtual storage a DIRECT ACCESS STORAGE DEVICE used to store programs that require more space than is available in main memory while they are executing: although the program appears to be held entirely in main memory, only those segments that are currently being used are so held. PAGING is a method by which virtual storage is used

virtual storage access method an ACCESS METHOD in which fixed–length or variable–length records are stored on a DIRECT ACCESS STORAGE DEVICE in **key sequence, entry sequence,** or **record–number sequence.** Records stored in key sequence are accessed according to a unique key, such as an employee number; in entry sequence, they are accessed in the order in which they are stored; in record–number sequence, they are accessed by a relative record number

visual display terminal a CRT or other type of screen used for viewing data, usually with an attached keyboard for entering data

VLSI abbreviation for VERY LARGE SCALE INTEGRATION the amount of integration on a chip comprising 100,000 or more gates: such chips are designed for use in microprocessors Compare SSI, MSI, LSI

voice–grade channel in data communications, a channel with a relatively narrow bandwidth, such as a telephone line, that is capable of transmitting human voice tones and that is used to transmit data at approximately 2500 bits per second to and from lower-speed devices, such as remote terminals and card readers Compare BROADBAND CHANNEL, NARROWBAND CHANNEL

voice output computer output in the form of prerecorded spoken words that are produced in response to the appropriate inquiry: for example, in banking systems, personnel can dial a phone number that connects them with the computer, enter an inquiry through a Touch-Tone keyboard, and receive a spoken response on the status of a customer's account

voice recognition the recognition by a computer of an individual's voice: the distinctive speech patterns of individuals are stored and matched against those input at a later time for identification

voice synthesizer see SPEECH SYNTHESIS

volatile designating main memory that does not retain data when the power supply is disconnected Compare NONVOLATILE

volatile file a file that has a high rate of additions and deletions of records Compare STATIC FILE

volatility 1 the potential loss of data from a storage device when the power is turned off **2** the relative number of additions to and deletions from a file

volume a removable storage medium, such as a reel of magnetic tape or a disk pack

volume label a record written at the beginning of a magnetic tape identifying the name or number assigned to the tape reel

volume table of contents VTOC

VRC abbreviation for VERTICAL REDUNDANCY CHECK a parity check on the bits contained in each transmitted character of a message Compare LRC, CRC

VSAM (VEE sam) acronym for **V**IRTUAL **S**TORAGE **A**CCESS **M**ETHOD

VTOC (VEE tock) acronym for **V**OLUME **T**ABLE **O**F **C**ONTENTS a table stored on a disk pack that contains the data set names and other descriptive information about each data set stored on the pack: the VTOC contains such information as the creation and expiration dates of the data set, its size and storage locations, the number of times it has been accessed, and the last date it was accessed

W

wafer a thin piece of silicon on which integrated circuits are formed to create a CHIP

wait state a phase during the execution of a program in which execution is interrupted while an input/output operation is performed

wand **1** a hand–held device resembling a pencil, used for reading magnetic characters, bar codes, and the like **2** LIGHT PEN

warm start the IPL of a computer in which jobs waiting to execute and waiting to print and various other data concerning the system are preserved so that processing can begin where it left off when the computer was brought down Compare COLD START

weighted designating a binary code in which a value has been assigned to each bit position. The values assigned to each position containing a binary 1 can be added together to determine the corresponding hexadecimal or decimal value of the bits· for example, in a four–bit code weighted from left to right as 8–4–2–1, the binary code of 1010 would equal a decimal value of 10 and a hexadecimal value of A

wideband channel BROADBAND CHANNEL

Winchester disk a DIRECT ACCESS STORAGE DEVICE that uses hard disks of 5 1/4, 8, or 14 inches in diameter which cannot be removed: the device is airtight and the read–write heads are lightly pressed against the disk, which is lubricated, thereby increasing its reliability since the head cannot crash onto the surface of the disk. Each individual disk can store approximately ten times more data, and provide a faster access time and transfer rate, than a comparably sized floppy disk: used with smaller computer systems

window a selected portion of a file or image displayed on a CRT

wire–matrix printer an IMPACT PRINTER that prints DOT–MATRIX CHARACTERS, one at a time, by pressing the ends of selected wires against an inked ribbon and paper: the wires are arranged in a 5x7, 7x7, or 7x9 rectangle

word **1** a storage unit, consisting of a number of bits usually determined when the machine is designed, that comprises one storage location in main memory: many minicomputers have 16–bit words, whereas a larger computer may have 32, 48, or 64 bits in each word See also VARIABLE WORD–LENGTH COMPUTER **2** the name used for a variable or constant in a program **3** the data value occupying a storage location

word–addressable designating a computer in which each word has a unique address that can be used in a program to access data Compare BYTE–ADDRESSABLE

word length the number of bits in a word: the word length is a multiple of the number of bytes: for example, if each byte contains eight bits, then the word length could be 16, or two bytes per word. The word length can be a fixed or variable number of bits See FIXED WORD-LENGTH COMPUTER, VARIABLE WORD-LENGTH COMPUTER

word mark see VARIABLE WORD-LENGTH COMPUTER

word-oriented computer a WORD-ADDRESSABLE computer

word processor an automated, computerized system incorporating variously an electronic typewriter, CRT terminal, memory, printer, and the like: it is used to prepare, edit, store, transmit, or duplicate letters, reports, records, etc., as for a business. Some programs now have spelling and syllabification verifiers

word time the time required to move a WORD from one storage location to another

work area WORKING STORAGE (sense 1)

working set the smallest set of instructions and data that should be together in main memory for the efficient processing of a program: this set changes in content and size as the execution progresses

working storage **1** a number of storage locations in main memory reserved for the data upon which operations are being performed **2** that part of a COBOL program used to assign names and attributes to such storage locations

work space WORKING STORAGE (sense 1)

wraparound **1** the automatic extension of a line of text onto two or more lines due to limitations of the display area **2** the continuation of data at the top of a CRT screen when the last position on the bottom of the screen has been filled **3** a return to the first addressable location in memory when the last addressable location has been used during an operation

write 1 to record data on a storage medium **2** the process of recording data Compare READ

write head an electromagnetic device used to record data on a magnetic storage device, such as magnetic tape or disk Compare READ HEAD

write–only designating main memory storage locations or stored files that can have data written into them but from which data cannot be read Compare READ–ONLY

WS abbreviation for WORKING STORAGE

X

xerographic printer a printer in which the paper is electrically charged on the areas that are to represent the characters and dusted with dry ink particles which adhere to the charged areas: the characters are then imprinted by a combination of heat and pressure, producing sharp images at the rate of approximately 400 lines per minute

XOR in a program, a LOGICAL OPERATOR connecting two propositions, each of which may be either true or false, that results in a new proposition. If one proposition is true and the other proposition is false, the new proposition is true; if both propositions are true or if both are false, the new proposition is false: for example, in the statement, "IF A=1 XOR B=1 THEN C=1," A=1 must be true and B=1 must be false (or vice versa) for C to equal one. If A and B both equal one or neither A nor B equals one, then C equals zero

XOR gate a gate that produces a signal of binary 0 when both input signals are 1 or both input signals are 0; otherwise the output signal is 1

X-punch ELEVEN-PUNCH

x-y plotter PLOTTER

Y

yoke a pair or group of READ-WRITE HEADS that are fastened together and move as a unit over two or more adjacent tracks on magnetic tape or disk

Y-punch TWELVE-PUNCH

Z

zap to erase a portion of a program, generally a machine language program, and, usually, replace it with other instructions

zero bit the leftmost HIGH-ORDER BIT in a word or byte: in some computers, the zero bit in the PRO-GRAM COUNTER is set to one when the ACCUMULA-TOR is cleared

zerofill to use zeros as CHARACTER FILL

zeroize ZEROFILL

zero punch a punch in the third row, called the zero-row, of an 80-COLUMN CARD See ZONE PUNCH

zero suppression the replacement with blanks of insignificant (that is, leading) zeros in a number so that they do not appear when the number is printed: for example, 00000751 would appear as 751

zone 1 a section of main memory reserved for a particular function or use **2** the top three rows on some punch cards

zone bits 1 in the eight–bit EBCDIC, the four left-most bits that are used to represent one or more ZONE PUNCHES: the four rightmost bits are used to represent one or more DIGIT PUNCHES **2** the four bits that are to the extreme left of a byte stored in ZONE DECIMAL

zone decimal the representation of a decimal number in one or more eight–bit bytes, where the rightmost four bits of each byte represent a digit and the leftmost four bits represent the zone bits: the zone bits for each digit are all 1111 (hexadecimal F), except for the zone bits of the rightmost byte, which contains the sign of the number. The zone bits for a plus sign are 1100 (hexadecimal C) and 1101 (hexadecimal D) for a minus sign: for example, the number –111 is represented in zone decimal as 1111 0001 1111 0001 1101 0001 or the hexadecimal equivalent of F1 F1 D1

zone punch a punched hole in any of the first three rows, called the **twelve–row, eleven–row,** and **zero–row,** respectively, of an 80-COLUMN CARD: the letters A through I are represented by a zone punch in the twelve–row and a digit punch in one of the rows 1 through 9; the letters J through R are represented by a zone punch in the eleven–row and a digit punch in one of the rows 1 through 9; the letters S through Z are represented by a zone punch in the zero–row and a digit punch in one of the rows 2 through 9 See HOLLERITH CODE Compare DIGIT PUNCH

CONVERSION TABLES

DECIMAL	BINARY	HEXADECIMAL	OCTAL
0	0000	0	0
1	0001	1	1
2	0010	2	2
3	0011	3	3
4	0100	4	4
5	0101	5	5
6	0110	6	6
7	0111	7	7
8	1000	8	10
9	1001	9	11
10	1010	A	12
11	1011	B	13
12	1100	C	14
13	1101	D	15
14	1110	E	16
15	1111	F	17
16	1 0000	10	20
17	1 0001	11	21
18	1 0010	12	22
19	1 0011	13	23
20	1 0100	14	24
21	1 0101	15	25
22	1 0110	16	26
23	1 0111	17	27
24	1 1000	18	30
25	1 1001	19	31
26	1 1010	1A	32
27	1 1011	1B	33
28	1 1100	1C	34
29	1 1101	1D	35
30	1 1110	1E	36
40	10 1000	28	50
50	11 0010	32	62

HEXADECIMAL AND DECIMAL CONVERSION

HEXADECIMAL COLUMNS

	6	5		4		3		2		1	
hex	dec	hex	dec	hex	dec	hex	dec	hex	dec	hex	dec
0	0	0	0	0	0	0	0	0	0	0	0
1	1,048,576	1	65,536	1	4,096	1	256	1	16	1	1
2	2,097,152	2	131,072	2	8,192	2	512	2	32	2	2
3	3,145,728	3	196,608	3	12,288	3	768	3	48	3	3
4	4,194,304	4	262,144	4	16,384	4	1,024	4	64	4	4
5	5,242,880	5	327,680	5	20,480	5	1,280	5	80	5	5
6	6,291,456	6	393,216	6	24,576	6	1,536	6	96	6	6
7	7,340,032	7	458,752	7	28,672	7	1,792	7	112	7	7
8	8,388,608	8	524,288	8	32,768	8	2,048	8	128	8	8
9	9,437,184	9	589,824	9	36,864	9	2,304	9	144	9	9
A	10,485,760	A	655,360	A	40,960	A	2,560	A	160	A	10
B	11,534,336	B	720,896	B	45,056	B	2,816	B	176	B	11
C	12,582,912	C	786,432	C	49,152	C	3,072	C	192	C	12
D	13,631,488	D	851,968	D	53,248	D	3,328	D	208	D	13
E	14,680,064	E	917,504	E	57,344	E	3,584	E	224	E	14
F	15,728,640	F	983,040	F	61,440	F	3,840	F	240	F	15

FROM HEXADECIMAL TO DECIMAL:

– Find each hexadecimal digit in the correct column position.

– Record corresponding decimal value for the digits in each position.

– Add the decimal values together to find the final decimal number.

For example, to find the decimal equivalent of the hexadecimal number A4BC, find the hexadecimal number A in the fourth column and record the decimal equivalent of 40,960; find the hexadecimal number 4 in the third column and record the decimal equivalent of 1,024; find the hexadecimal number B in the second column and record the decimal equivalent of 176; find the hexadecimal number C in the first column and record the decimal equivalent of 12. Adding the decimal numbers together results in a total of 42,172—the decimal equivalent of A4BC.

FROM DECIMAL TO HEXADECIMAL:

– Find the largest decimal number in the table that is less than the number to be converted.

– Record its hexadecimal equivalent.

– Subtract the number found in the table from the number to be converted.

– Repeat the process until there is no remainder.

For example, to find the hexadecimal equivalent of the decimal number 41,540, find in the table the number closest to but not exceeding 41,540, which is 40,960. Record the corresponding hexadecimal digit of A. Subtract 40,960 from 41,540. Find in the table the closest number to the remainder 580 that does not exceed 580, which is 512. Record the corresponding hexadecimal digit of 2. Subtract 512 from 580. Look in the table again for the remainder of 68. Find 64 in the table, record the hexadecimal digit 4, and subtract 64 from 68. Look in the last column for the remainder of 4 and record the hexadecimal digit 4. Arranging the digits in order from left to right results in the hexadecimal number A244, which is the hexadecimal equivalent of 41,540.

POWERS OF TWO TABLE

n	2^n
0	1
1	2
2	4
3	8
4	16
5	32
6	64
7	128
8	256
9	512
10	1 024
11	2 048
12	4 096
13	8 192
14	16 384
15	32 768

POWERS OF SIXTEEN TABLE

n	16^n
0	1
1	16
2	256
3	4 096
4	65 536
5	1 048 576
6	16 777 216
7	268 435 456
8	4 294 967 296
9	68 719 476 736
10	1 099 511 627 776
11	17 592 186 044 416
12	281 474 976 710 656
13	4 503 599 627 370 496
14	72 057 594 037 927 936
15	1 152 921 504 606 846 976

THE EBCDIC CHARACTER SET

	CHARACTER	BINARY		HEX
LETTERS:	A	1100	0001	C1
	B	1100	0010	C2
	C	1100	0011	C3
	D	1100	0100	C4
	E	1100	0101	C5
	F	1100	0110	C6
	G	1100	0111	C7
	H	1100	1000	C8
	I	1100	1001	C9
	J	1101	0001	D1
	K	1101	0010	D2
	L	1101	0011	D3
	M	1101	0100	D4
	N	1101	0101	D5
	O	1101	0110	D6
	P	1101	0111	D7
	Q	1101	1000	D8
	R	1101	1001	D9
	S	1110	0010	E2
	T	1110	0011	E3
	U	1110	0100	E4
	V	1110	0101	E5
	W	1110	0110	E6
	X	1110	0111	E7
	Y	1110	1000	E8
	Z	1110	1001	E9
DIGITS:	0	1111	0000	F0
	1	1111	0001	F1
	2	1111	0010	F2
	3	1111	0011	F3
	4	1111	0100	F4
	5	1111	0101	F5
	6	1111	0110	F6
	7	1111	0111	F7
	8	1111	1000	F8
	9	1111	1001	F9

	CHARACTER	BINARY		HEX
SPECIAL SYMBOLS:	,	0110	1011	6B
	=	0111	1110	7E
	(	0100	1101	4D
	)	0101	1101	5D
	−	0110	0000	60
	.	0100	1011	4B
	/	0110	0001	61
	'	0111	1101	7D
	<	0100	1100	4C
	>	0110	1110	6E
	$	0101	1011	5B
	¢	0100	1010	4A
	%	0110	1100	6C
	+	0100	1110	4E
	:	0111	1010	7A
	;	0101	1110	5E
	*	0101	1100	5C
	"	0111	1111	7F
	_	0110	1101	6D
	@	0111	1100	7C
	¬	0101	1111	5F
	&	0101	0000	50
	#	0111	1011	7B
	!	0101	1010	5A
	?	0110	1111	6F
			0100	1111	4F

THE ASCII CHARACTER SET

	CHARACTER	BINARY		HEX
LETTERS:	A	0100	0001	41
	B	0100	0010	42
	C	0100	0011	43
	D	0100	0100	44
	E	0100	0101	45
	F	0100	0110	46
	G	0100	0111	47
	H	0100	1000	48
	I	0100	1001	49
	J	0100	1010	4A
	K	0100	1011	4B
	L	0100	1100	4C
	M	0100	1101	4D
	N	0100	1110	4E
	O	0100	1111	4F
	P	0101	0000	50
	Q	0101	0001	51
	R	0101	0010	52
	S	0101	0011	53
	T	0101	0100	54
	U	0101	0101	55
	V	0101	0110	56
	W	0101	0111	57
	X	0101	1000	58
	Y	0101	1001	59
	Z	0101	1010	5A
DIGITS:	0	0011	0000	30
	1	0011	0001	31
	2	0011	0010	32
	3	0011	0011	33
	4	0011	0100	34
	5	0011	0101	35
	6	0011	0110	36
	7	0011	0111	37
	8	0011	1000	38
	9	0011	1001	39

THE ASCII CHARACTER SET
(continued)

	CHARACTER	BINARY		HEX
SPECIAL				
SYMBOLS:	,	0010	1100	2C
	=	0011	1101	3D
	(	0010	1000	28
	)	0010	1001	29
	−	0010	1101	2D
	.	0010	1110	2E
	/	0010	1111	2F
	'	0010	0111	27
	<	0011	1100	3C
	>	0011	1110	3E
	$	0010	0100	24
	%	0010	0101	25
	+	0010	1011	2B
	:	0011	1010	3A
	;	0011	1011	3B
	*	0010	1010	2A
	"	0010	0010	22
	_	0101	1111	5F
	@	0100	0000	40
	¬	0101	1110	5E
	&	0010	0110	26
	#	0010	0011	23
	!	0010	0001	21
	?	0011	1111	3F
	|	0010	0001	21